Naming the God

In paganism the gods are at the center of our magick. They are our parents, our friends, and even our children at times. They connect us to the energies of the Universe that transform us. There are so many gods available it can be difficult to know which one speaks to us. *Naming the God* is a wonderful anthology that teaches us the different types of gods we can work with. From Sun Gods to Dark Gods and on to Shamanic Gods, this book give you the insight you will need to connect to the god that is calling out to you!

Chris Allaun, *Author of Otherworld: Ecstatic Spirits of the Land and A Guide of Spirits: A Psychopomp's Manual for Transitioning the Dead to the Afterlife*

A wide-ranging series of essays on approaching the deities as a modern pagan, thought-provoking and informative. Ideal to dip into or as a first stop before setting off into deeper research.

Fiona Dove, Shaman Teacher and Runemaster

If you are wishing to connect to or discover how to create a solid, working relationship with, the old Gods, the Ancient ones, this book provides both personal experiences and well informed listings, to inspire your search.

Kim McMuldrow, Shaman and Horse-whisperer

Naming the God is a collection of fascinating essays about the many male deities that have been worshipped by different cultures and civilisations around the world. There are gods from the past and present, gods from the east and west, gods from the north and south, gods of the shamans, gods of every

type known! If you want to find out about gods this is the book to read!
Steve Andrews, Author of *Herbs of the Sun, Moon and Planets*

Fascinating perspectives on divine masculine archetypes and gods, and introductions to some wonderful gods. Not just the usual suspects either!
Halo Quin, Author of *Gods and Goddesses of Wales*

This collection offers a wide ranging introduction to deity across a broad spectrum of paths. Presented in two sections, looking at both different types of deities and an alphabetized list of deities from across the world. It should prove a handy reference guide for beginners and those who wish to explore a range of deities that may currently be unfamiliar to them.
Luke Eastwood, Author of *The Druid's Primer*, *The Journey* and *Kerry Folk Tales*

Naming the God

Naming the God

Edited by Trevor Greenfield

**MOON
BOOKS**

Winchester, UK
Washington, USA

JOHN HUNT PUBLISHING

First published by Moon Books, 2022
Moon Books is an imprint of John Hunt Publishing Ltd., No. 3 East Street, Alresford
Hampshire SO24 9EE, UK
office@jhpbooks.net
www.johnhuntpublishing.com
www.moon-books.net

For distributor details and how to order please visit the 'Ordering' section on our website.

Text copyright: Trevor Greenfield 2021

ISBN: 978 1 78904 455 3
978 1 78904 456 0 (ebook)
Library of Congress Control Number: 2021934881

A CIP catalogue record for this book is available from the British Library.

Design: Stuart Davies

UK: Printed and bound by CPI Group (UK) Ltd, Croydon, CR0 4YY
Printed in North America by CPI GPS partners

We operate a distinctive and ethical publishing philosophy in
all areas of our business, from our global network of authors to
production and worldwide distribution.

Contents

Preface

In 2014 Moon Books published *Naming the Goddess*. As a new kid on the block in Pagan publishing, we had decided from the outset to be community focused and bring out anthologies to which many people could contribute. Over eighty people contributed to *Naming the Goddess* and it was considered by many to be a great success. The obvious follow-up was *Naming the God*, a companion volume for its well-received sister. Time flies, other projects took over and the idea was shelved with other books published instead.

But you can't keep a good idea down... its time would come and its time has come. Moon Books is, at last, proud to present *Naming the God*.

Part 1

Writing the God

Working with the Gods

Rachel Patterson

As a Pagan Witch, working with deity has been part of my pathway from the beginning. Probably around thirty years now, which makes me feel very old! However, my view of deity may be different to the next witch. My thoughts are this; the divine is like a huge single diamond. Each facet is a different deity, with their own individual persona. But the sum of the parts makes up the whole. The source is one – male, female, neither, both.

One of the first areas of study for me was to find a pantheon to work with. There is a dizzying array to choose from. In the end I started with the Celts, as I live in England it made most sense to me. I researched a huge list of names, being drawn to one or two along the way. But interestingly now I think about it, the majority were goddesses rather than gods. It also seems that throughout my journey the feminine has been represented far more than the masculine.

As my journey twisted and turned, I have ended up working with deities from all different pantheons across the globe. Some have stayed for a short while, others longer. Again, most of them seem to be goddesses. The ancient British goddess, The Cailleach has been with me for many years now in fact.

But what about gods? Going back a few years I took a course, written by a very lovely male witch. The course focused on the masculine. I was excited as I felt unbalanced somehow, just working with the goddess and was looking forward to new discoveries. The course was designed to help meet a god to work with. But perhaps because I hate following rules, I didn't meet a god at all. What I did find was a male spirit animal guide and my wild boar side kick has been with me ever since. So, although it was an interesting experience exploring the masculine, I still came away without a god to work with.

As Witches we focus a lot on balance, working with light and dark. The moon and the sun, above and below and all four elements. Although it does seem we work more with the moon than perhaps we do with the sun? Do we focus too much on the feminine? In deity form as the goddess and her energy as the moon?

There are countless courses and books on working with the goddess and some covens that only work with a feminine energy. Are there the same for the gods? I am not so sure.

Obviously, religion has taken its toll. We moved to a patriarchy a good while back now (no, I am not old enough to remember the beginning of it). And I think that has had an adverse effect on how we see deity now. In recent years there has been a huge shift to move to a system headed by the feminine. However, I do worry that we have moved from a very one sided male orientated system and are pushing to have an equally one-sided female one. What about somewhere in between?

In more recent years, for me it has been an exploration to find balance. I have actively sought out the god energy. But it seemed to be brief fleeting connections with each god. In the end I realized I was trying too hard. Then, when I wasn't looking, a male deity sought me. I do believe that is how it is meant to be. However, I didn't recognize the signs at first, or maybe I did, and I was just playing hard to get…

Elephants…everywhere. I couldn't turn around without falling over them. Obviously not real elephants because that would be really weird. But images of them on TV, in books, magazines and on billboards and every shop I visited seemed to have elephant ornaments and fabrics. Then I had a light bulb moment. Lord Ganesha was literally shouting his trunk off at me. Several meditations later I had myself a strong Ganesha connection. He was with me for several years. An altar appeared in his honour to which I made daily offerings and his support and guidance were invaluable. But eventually he slipped out of my life, his work having been completed. I am very thankful for his presence and I still maintain a small altar to him even though I don't work with him on a regular basis now.

So, I was adrift again, working only with The Cailleach, albeit that her strength and support are incredibly important to me. She is enough to kick my butt when I need it. But I do like that balance. And she wasn't actually very tolerant of the elephant headed god interfering to be honest! A realization dawned, that I had started to work a lot more with the energy of the sun. Duh! That was the masculine energy I was seeking... Without even thinking about it, I had been providing the balance all along.

From that moment of breakthrough something else happened. A god peeped in, like a ray of sun through the clouds (pun completely intended). The Celtic god, Belenus showed his face.

Ridiculously, I had known about him for years, on my visits to the royal city of Bath in Somerset, England, where he has a presence. But maybe the time wasn't right before?

He fits. He is the summer to my goddess' winter. He is the sun to her moon. And although it doesn't bother me about mixing pantheons, he happens to be from the Celtic pantheon. The Cailleach actually being seriously old and pre-Celt, but she is happy to share with a more 'close to home' god. When I say happy, I mean she tolerates him. It has been a perfect pairing.

Now, that's a bit of insight into my own personal experience, but it will be different for everyone. My advice when working or looking to work with any deity:

- Explore. Don't feel restricted to one pantheon or even just your 'local' deities. There is big wide world out there packed full of gods for you to investigate.
- Research, research, research. Do your homework. It pays to know who you are dealing with. If you are looking for a god to assist with a particular intent, make sure that it

comes within their remit. You don't want to call upon a god of war to help with a love spell. Learn about their culture. A lot of deities have specific rituals and blessings to follow. The Hindu deities for instance, each god has particular ways of being honoured. Learn about them, read their myths and stories.

- Respect. Mind your manners. Treat each deity with respect. Ask, don't demand. They are not your servants.
- Be thankful. Remember to give thanks, offerings are good and paying them attention is perfect. Think carefully about what you want in return. Are you giving an offering because you have asked for something or are you just honouring the god? You cannot keep taking and expecting help and results without giving something back.
- Offerings. Making offerings in thanks or to honour a god is excellent. However, make sure you have done your research. A god of wine probably won't appreciate a glass of orange juice. And please, please, please be mindful. If you are making offerings outside, make sure they are biodegradable.
- Listen and learn. Easier said than done, believe me I know. If a god is shouting for your attention, there will be a very good reason for it. Pay heed.
- Mix and match. Personal experience has taught me that most deities from different pantheons do work together. Just be mindful that some won't.
- Trust your intuition. If you feel drawn to a deity, go with it. Learn to trust your inner self and be guided by your intuition, it won't let you down. And in complete disagreement with my statement above, if you feel your intuition is guiding you to give the god of wine a glass of fruit juice – do it! Who knows? He may need it to cure a hangover.
- Once you find a god to work with, or one finds you, make

a connection. I find meditating with the intent of meeting them is a good first step. Be guided by their messages.

- If the god is going to be around for a while, I like to add something to my altar to represent them. Or if I feel guided to do so, I create an altar solely for them.

- When you make a real solid connection with a god and you feel you are called to do their work, it can be very rewarding. You may well take on their values and a lot of your actions will be guided by their virtues.

- Remember that sometimes a god will require you to sacrifice something or push yourself outside of your comfort zone. I am not talking about taking a life (good grief!) or making you do something you believe to be morally or legally wrong. But I have found that the gods do know best and to enable us to achieve our potential and reach our goals they may want you to really push yourself. Nobody said this was going to be easy!

- There are different levels for each of us to work with the gods. You might only work with a god for a specific goal or intent. You may dedicate your life work to a particular god. Or anywhere in between. Each of us is different and our journeys are individual. Your 'working with a god' will probably be completely different to my working with them.

- I have used the phrase 'working with' because that is how I feel about it. I am not equal to my gods, but I do work with them as I would work with a boss. I do their work, I do what they ask, not always without a struggle...I trust that they know what is right for me. You might choose to call it 'worshipping the gods.' There is nothing wrong with that phrase at all, they have earnt the right to be worshipped.

- You are in control. If you feel the call from a god but you really don't want to work with them. Tell them. Be polite, no need for rudeness. But trust your intuition. If it all feels hinky then don't do it.

- Keep your promises. If you have made a connection to a god and promised to work with them. Keep to it. Making a commitment, because that's exactly what it is, and it can sometimes be difficult to stick to. But it pays you to honour your promise.

- My word of caution. Some deities are a tad mischievous. If you are drawn to work with some of the more 'adventurous' gods, Loki is a good example, be prepared. I am not saying it is a bad thing to work with him, or that it won't be worth it. Just remember he brings a bit of chaos with him that will shake your life up. A shake up could be just what you need but forewarned is forearmed, as they say.

There is a definite difference in energy with the gods from the goddess. Although each individual has their own unique character. The masculine and feminine bring their own energy to the table. Bringing them together helps me find a sense of balance.

Then of course not all the gods are specifically male or female. There are a lot that are dual gender or neither. The gods provide us with a beautifully diverse palette to work with. It must be right for you. You may find working with a dual gender or non-specific gender deity on their own suits you perfectly. You might find that working with two goddesses or two gods is more you. You may prefer to just work with one god or one goddess. You might even dismiss deity completely and just work with the spirit of the place or Father Sun and Mother Moon (or vice versa, as I say, who am I to judge?). This is your journey. Only you know what fits in with your spiritual adventure. There is no right or wrong.

Finding that perfect balance is important to me, particularly in this mad world we live in. It matters not to me what gender you are or identify with (it is not my business to judge). It matters not what colour your skin or hair. It matters not to me what country you were born in. I don't care what you wear or don't wear. It does matter to me how you treat yourself, other people and the environment. To me, that is all that is important. We are all on this same planet, we need to stop fighting each other and come together – as human beings (and aliens, I don't judge). We need to care for each other and our world. The gods and our spiritual beliefs can help us do this, by providing balance, support, strength and guidance. Let's help the gods, to help us sort out this crazy mess we are in.

Rachel Patterson is High Priestess of the Kitchen Witch Coven and an Elder of the Kitchen Witch School of Natural Witchcraft. A Hedge/Kitchen Witch with an added dash of folk magic, she is also the author of a number of books including *Kitchen Witchcraft*, *Moon Magic* and *A Kitchen Witch's World of Magical Plants & Herbs*.

Trickster Gods

Andrew Anderson

Psst! Are you bored of all those 'holier than thou' deities, the ones that always seem to be saving the world and banging on about things like morality, covenants, service, that sort of thing? Well, step this way, because you've found the fun stuff. Welcome to the world of the trickster Gods. They've got it all! Feathery arson! Bum punishment! Hat trickery! Trickster Gods really know how to have a good time and that, frankly, is why we love them. Oh, come on, don't go all pious on me now! You love them, despite yourself! Yes, they may have been stifled under monotheistic, Abrahamic religions for a couple of centuries, but they have been finding their way back into our hearts from the moment we were told that we shouldn't trust them.

Everybody loves a bad boy, right? Just look at the presentation of Loki in the Marvel Cinematic Universe. Tom Hiddleston's meddlesome Demi-god has become one of the standout characters, even reaching beyond the movies and into his own TV mini-series. Similarly, Anansi and Wisakedjak have found new life as Mr Nancy and Whiskey Jack in Neil Gaiman's novel and the TV series, *American Gods*. And what about Dwayne 'The Rock' Johnson's Maui from Disney's *Moana*? Then, of course, there is 'the Daddy' of them all, the one who has used every trick in the book over the last 2,000 years to get himself into movies, novels, TV shows, epic poetry … but, more about him later.

So, what is it that makes the trickster Gods so engaging? Well, a big part of their charm is that they behave like a bunch of big kids. That childlike quality helps them create situations which are not only disorderly but often outright chaotic. They grab us by our inner child and run us around the playground of the universe. They become our silly, scatological best friend who we cheer on, even though we know we shouldn't. Take Wisakedjak, hero of the Algonquin and Cree tribes, for example, who grew so annoyed that his farts were making his arrows miss their target that he punished his own bum by sticking it in a fire. Or Loki, who cut off Sif's beautiful long hair while she slept, just because he thought it would be funny. Or part-time Celtic trickster Lugh, whose shape changing abilities may have been the root of the stories about those naughty little Leprechauns. Admit it, those stories made you smile, didn't they? Particularly the one about Wisakedjak's bum (you wait until you hear about how he ended up eating his bum scabs, thinking they were dried meat!). And that's the point. We love tricksters because they make us smile and laugh, even if we disapprove of what they are doing.

While it would be correct to say that Tricksters are child-like, we could equally say that they are, in fact, incredibly selfish. I mean, yes, it is funny to shave off someone's hair as they sleep but it's not a particularly nice thing to do. And it is true; tricksters are usually very self-centred. They do what they want and do not listen to the warnings of others. In that sense, they embody the very spirit of the individual as it battles against the straight-jacket of community and society. Like James Dean, they are rebels without a cause. They are punks, hanging around on street corners and spitting on the floor of social convention. Oh, how we cross our arms and tut in disapproval, but deep inside we get a little thrill at the thought of the anarchy they incite. Besides, through their antics, Tricksters deliver a big old dollop of moral ambiguity. They may have acted selfishly but that doesn't mean that the ends don't benefit everyone. Take Eshu, the trickster God of the Yoruba people, for example. In one of his most divisive antics, Eshu walked down the middle of a street wearing a hat that was white on one side and black on the other. He then waited while disagreements erupted between people on different sides of the street about what colour the hat was. When the disagreements were at fever pitch, Eshu returned, turned his hat inside out, and showed them that the hat was in fact red! What began as a selfish act on Eshu's part became a valuable lesson to the people on the street (and anyone who has ever been on social media).

Because they are acting from a place of self-centredness and self-fulfilment, tricksters are often associated with the act of temptation. They can either tempt others into committing a transgression or they can be motivated by temptation themselves. A perfect example of this is master storyteller and child of the Earth and Sky, Anansi, the spider. For example, in the tale where Anansi wants to buy all of the stories in the world from his father, Nyame, he is sent on a quest to capture several dangerous beasts. Anansi uses his cunning to position each of the creatures in a difficult situation and then tempts them with an easy solution. Each time, the beast falls for his tempting trick and he captures them, ultimately gaining all of the stories in the world from Nyame. This sense of tempting others into a mistake is found in many trickster tales, such as when Hercules tempts Atlas into putting the world back on his shoulders, supposedly temporarily, before running off with the golden apples of Hesperides. Conversely, Anansi is also an example of a trickster who is frequently tempted himself. For example, having won all of the stories in the world from Nyame, Anansi is tempted to hoard all the wisdom in the world. He collects it up, crams in in a pot and sets out to hide it high in a tree. However, tricked by his son Ntikuma, Anansi drops the pot and his wisdom is distributed to all the peoples of the world. Temptation, whether used by the trickster as a device or pursued as a motive, often leads to trouble.

Anansi's trump card is his amazing ability to communicate, to tell stories and entrance listeners, and he is not the only trickster with the gift of the gab. Both the Greek trickster Hermes and his Roman equivalent Mercury are messengers of the Gods, presiding over communication. Narada, from the Hindu pantheon, has a similar role as messenger, as does Eshu, who knows all of the languages of humankind. In fact, Eshu was so convincing that he once persuaded the Sun and Moon to change places and completely upset the natural order of the universe! Interestingly, Mercury, Hermes and Eshu are also connected to the worlds of commerce. Whether buying a used car or digital currency, we need to keep our eye out for such tricksters. If that deal looks too good to be true, it probably is.

While some tricksters may be trying to sell you something you don't need, others have given humanity something incredibly valuable. In mythology from around the world there is a strong connection between tricksters and the gift of fire. Perhaps the most well-known, in Western culture, is the Greek Titan Prometheus who, after forming humankind from clay and water, stole Zeus' fire and snuck it out of Olympus in a stalk of Fennel. Similarly, one of the tales about Maui tells how he brought fire from Mahuika, while in Micronesian mythology, it is the trickster Olifat who gets a bird to bring fire to humanity from the sun. One common Australian Aboriginal Myth tells how the trickster Crow stole fire from guardians in the Dreamtime, ultimately causing much of the land to be scorched and colouring his feathers ashy black.

Some tricksters don't need to steal fire from anywhere else; they have the potential for ignition in the palms of their hands. Twisted fire starters such as these tricksters are Gods of thunder and lightning. In Norse mythology it isn't Loki but Thor who is God of thunder, although he does get involved in several scrapes with Loki, notably doing full drag to convince Thrym that he was the beautiful potential bride, Freya. King of the Hindu Gods Indra is a powerful trickster who wields a weapon made from the spine of another God, Dadichi, which sparks with thunder and lightning. The mischievous Slavic God Veles, a shapeshifter and magician, is said to repeatedly challenge the storm god Perun. Both Indra and Veles have roles as guardians of the Underworld, which is shared by Celtic trickster Manannán Mac Lir. While he doesn't command thunder and lightning, Manannán Mac Lir is the God of the sea, a perfect domain for a changeable and unpredictable trickster.

It is the rumblings and explosions, the currents and eddies of a very different force which preoccupy another bunch of tricksters. We could be polite and use the word 'procreation' but that doesn't really cover it adequately, so let's just call it lust, shall we? There are some trickster Gods who are never happier than when they've got their phallus out and are waving it at passers-by. In fact, one of the ways the Greeks honoured horny old Hermes was to create a Herm, a large phallic sculpture with nothing but a human head on the top and a lovely set of male dangly bits sticking out the front. Well, I suppose it's somewhere to hang your hat. Hopi trickster and fertility God Kokopelli is often depicted as hunched over blowing his own flute (not a euphemism), while Aztec God and wily old dog Huehuecóyotl (no, I'm not being rude, his name literally means "Old Coyote") is not only a God of mischief but also of sexual passion. The mix of trickster and unbridled sexuality often leads to difficult and distressing acts. Take Welsh trickster Gwydion, for example. Son of the God Beli and Goddess Dôn, Gwydion actually causes a war so that his randy brother, Gilfaethwy can rape the virginal Goewin. As punishment, over a period of three years, Gwydion and Gilfaethwy are transformed into a mating pair of deer, boar and wolves, one male, one female. Each year they breed and their children are taken from them. The bestial punishment seems to work on Gwydion who continues his trickery but steers well clear of any further sexual entanglements – unless you count his creation of the flower maiden Blodeuwedd who he expects will remain loyal to his nephew Lleu (spoiler: she doesn't).

Gwydion and Gilfaethwy's transformation into various

beasts, shepherds us towards a major group of tricksters in pantheons from around the world – those who appear in the form of animals. We've already encountered many of them in this article. Charismatic trickster Anansi, whose stories emerged in Africa but are now told all over the world, is a spider. That cheeky Aboriginal Crow, still covered in the ashes and soot of the fire he started, has become the inspiration for various pieces of English Literature, namely Ted Hughes' poetry collection *Crow* and Max Porter's astonishing work *Grief is the Thing with Feathers*. The indigenous people of the Pacific North West Coast have trickster Ravens while Raven and Coyote are the stars of many Native American tales. In China we find Sun Wukong, otherwise known as Monkey or the Monkey King, whose adventures are retold in the epic *Journey to the West*. Even the Celtic Bear God Artaois, who has associations with Gwydion and Mercury, may have had elements of the trickster about him.

So, why do so many tricksters appear as animals? Well, they represent the same, untamed wild energy that we find in our child-like tricksters. They encourage us and warn us about the primal energy we have within. They also remind us that we, humankind, are, essentially, animals ourselves. We are connected to the natural world and what we do has an effect. If we ever get too uppity, too proud, too distanced from our roots, we go back to those stories and find supposedly clever humans being outsmarted by mere 'dumb' animals.

Of course, there is one trickster I haven't mentioned yet. He was a relative latecomer to the party and yet we can regard him as the Daddy of them all. People have taken qualities from many different tricksters and attributed them all to him. He is a Romantic hero, the epitome of evil and, if you believe the makers of *South Park*, a Gay Icon. Who else could it be but the big man himself: The Beast, Abaddon, Lucifer, Satan, Mammon, the big bad Boogey Man. Yup, it's the Devil.

He is animalistic, often shown as a shaggy-haired beast with cloven hooves, a tail and horns. He is frequently depicted as being child-like, notably in woodcuts where he gets humans to kiss his bum or literally poops them out. Cheeky! Like some of our other tricksters, he is the God of the underworld and, while he may not have given humanity the gift of fire, he certainly seems to love toasting sinners on the flames of his fiery realm. Commerce is definitely his domain; money is, after all, the root of all evil. He has even been shown to have the gift of the gab; Milton's Satan in *Paradise Lost* creates "a heaven of hell, a hell of heaven" just through his words. He really is the master of Fake News. Thank goodness he doesn't have a Twitter account. Lust is one of the seven Deadly Sins, all of which seem to be in Satan's remit, and his skills as a tempter are legendary.

Yes, the Devil really is the arch trickster. His influence has been so pervasive that, when Eshu's name was first translated from Yoruba to English, it was translated as Satan. The Western, Christian perception of the Devil meant that other tricksters were damned with his name. Within a monotheistic belief system, where the main deity became everything that is perfect and good, the Devil's rebellion means he became far more than just a cheeky chappie; he became the epitome of evil itself. He was turned from being a trickster who, by leading humans from the path of righteousness, could make them realise something about themselves to something that should be shunned at all cost.

Not that we listened; we have been hailing Satan for centuries. He has become by far the most interesting character in many poems, novels, TV shows and films, even those that are supposedly meant to be warning us against him. We even dress our kids up as him on Halloween. And that's the point, we can dress tricksters up, denigrate them for thousands of years and warn against the dire consequences of following them, but they always stick with us, because they are a part of us. When we look at trickster Gods, we get a clearer reflection of ourselves than we do with the musclebound heroes, the elder sages or sacrificial lambs. It really is a case of "Better the Devil", or trickster, "you know"!

Andrew Anderson is a member of The Order of Bards, Ovates and Druids. He is a freelance Tutor, Celebrant, Theatre Director and Period Interpreter. He is the and author of *The Ritual of Writing* and *Artio and Artaois*.

Sun Gods

Mabh Savage

The weather is wild today. The sky looms yellow and sulphurous; iron clouds battling with the brass sun. As the metals clash, the sparks become snowflakes that whip wildly across my windscreen. It is a battle; the Sun God facing off against the enemy elements; a war as old as time itself.

As tiny primates scrabbling on the surface of a scorched, soaked and battered rock, we have tried, for millennia, to make sense of the wild and wonderful world around us. Why does the rain one year make the crops grow, and the next year cause the flood that washes them away? Why does the wind both gently pollinate the fruit trees, and also send them crashing into one another in a maelstrom of destruction?

It's only natural that we start to anthropomorphise these events, and even attribute human emotions to them. The wind must be angry! The rain is pleased with us this year! Eventually this animism of seasonal events is infected with our human need to weave tales and stories. The angry wind develops into the angry wind god, and suddenly the story isn't simply one of appeasing the seasons, but one of understanding the nature of the gods that lie behind the seasons; the spirits and deities that pull the strings. It's not enough to simply accept that the wind, the rain or the sun might be imbued with a personality. We crave understanding of the creation and life stories of these aspects of our universe. We want to know that these gods have had trials and tribulations just like us, because then we can relate to them, and we can understand them. Although we bow our heads to the dirt in worship, or dance secret dances, or burn sacred herbs, secretly we know that in many ways, the gods are just like us, and can, therefore, empathise with our plight.

This need to relate to our deities appears in most pantheons. The Greek pantheon is full of tales of love, jealousy, greed and all the things that we are perhaps a bit ashamed of in ourselves. The Egyptian pantheon is perhaps more removed from humanity, especially in the animal aspects of the gods. Still, we see tales of love and desire, and a connection between the earth and the sky which runs through most religions. Humans live on the earth and look up to the sky, for both life-giving rain and warming sunshine.

The Norse pantheon sees thunder and lightning given huge honour and respect, with tales of Thor known worldwide. Sól, the sun, sister of the moon is a little less well known. This makes sense when you think about where the Norse people came from, the weather and seasons there, and the fact that they were a seafaring race. Hailing from Scandinavia, where the sun hides for much of the year, it is no wonder Sol is not seen as powerful as some of the other gods or personifications. However, she is still vital and recognised as such. Conversely in Egypt, close to the equator where the sun burns hot, bright and magnificent, Ra (or Re) is one of the major gods and even seen as a creator god in some cults. Man was born from the spilled tears of Ra; a beautiful and simple metaphor for the fact that without sunlight and rain, we simply would not exist.

Whether crucial to the pantheon and its mythology or merely a minor player in the side lines, the sun god is an important part of theological history. Creating solar deities is an early step in trying to understand how the universe around us works. There are many versions of something pulling or pushing the sun across the sky, because how else would the sun rise and set each day? In Ancient Egypt, Ra was said to travel in two boats; the Mandjet and the Mesektet. These boats represented the morning and the evening. They took Ra on a journey across the sky during the daytime and into the underworld during the night. Another Ancient Egyptian god, Khepri, was supposed to push the sun across the sky in the form of a scarab beetle, just like the famous beetles pushed balls of dung. An artefact discovered in Denmark in 1902 appears to be a Bronze age statue of a horse pulling the sun on a wheeled chariot. The Trundholm Sun Chariot may date from 1400 BCE. Although the model appears to be indicative of a belief in a supernatural being pulling the sun across the sky, there are markings on the wheel surrounding the sun which may be evidence that this sculpture is a form of a six-month calendar. This could be a sign of the blending of religious beliefs and astronomical knowledge; early steps towards a more scientific way of looking at the sun and how it relates to the earth.

Sun gods are nearly always complex deities, much more than their association with the fiery orb at the centre of our universe. Ra wasn't just a sun god. Ra was a god of creation, of renewal and rebirth, and as part of this second aspect, linked with Osiris, the god of the underworld. The links between solar deities and gods of the dead might not seem obvious at first, but many religions are based around natural cycles. These include the changes of the seasons, life and death, and the rising and the setting of the sun. It's easy to conflate the sun rising each dawn and setting each dusk with the more primal human issues of life and death. Surely, then, it makes perfect sense that the God who has dominion over this vast change in the sky which is beyond our comprehension may have something to do with those other massive transitions in our lives. The dawning of our childhood, and the waning of our latter years is our own journey across the sky, and the God of one journey can easily become the god of the other.

The ancient Greeks had their own sun gods. The earliest was Helios, a crowned god who drove a chariot across the sky. It was common for Greek (and Roman) deities to have various epithets, or names. These described various aspects of the god and some, at times, become a separate entity with their own cult or temple. Helios was called Hyperion, which means "high"; Elektor which may mean beaming; Phaëton, which means radiant; Terpsimbrotos, the pleaser of mortals; and Hekatebolos, the far shooter of arrows, where the arrows represent the sun's rays. Helios had a small but crucial part to play in certain Greek myths which have latterly become very famous. The Homeric Hymn to Demeter tells the story of the kidnapping of Persephone (Kore). Hekate helps Persephone's mother, Demeter, and they go together to meet Helios. As the sun, he sees over the whole land, and is the only one to have noted where Persephone was taken. This all-seeing aspect is a common aspect of major gods and one that has remained constant throughout the ages. How many monotheistic religions still worship the idea of the omnipresent and omniscient God?

The role of the sun god was joined later by Apollo, another complex god, widely worshipped across Greece and later by the Romans. Phoebus Apollo was the epithet that made him a sun god: shining Apollo. Apollo was a literal archer, the rays of the sun becoming real arrows. Apollo also embraced the aforementioned all-seeing nature but in a different way. He became a god of prophecy and oracles, and was the deity of the Delphic Oracle, also called the Pythia. I recently visited a temple of Apollo on the island of Rhodes. I remember walking in between the ruined pillars, into the small rectangle temple space, and imagining the energy that would have flowed through here during the days of ritual and celebration. The small temple is part of a much larger complex. It has an almost buried amphitheatre and buildings which archaeologists from the Italian School of Archaeology at Athens believe would have been used to house guests from all over the island at times of festivals.

Of course, this temple is a tiny thing compared to the massive temple of Apollo in Rhodes Town. The small temple near our beautiful village of Theologos is of Apollo Erethimios, an epithet which may mean "averter of mildew" (Cecil Torr, 1885) which is certainly a valid, if minor, function of the sun; to keep things dry and safe from mouldering. The temple on the huge hill of the Akropolis is, despite being covered in scaffolding at the time we saw it, quite something. This temple is to Pythian Apollo, the prophetic aspect, and is the most visible and striking part of the acropolis. The Apollo temple wasn't the largest structure here; Athena and Zeus both had more impressive temples. However, Apollo wasn't the Rhodians first love affair with a Sun God. Their worship of the sun was so powerful they created one of the Seven Wonders of the Ancient World: The Colossus of Rhodes, an enormous statue of Helios. The statue represented victory in battle, showing how vital the ancient Greeks believed the sun to be in providing good fortune and blessing in warfare. An early taste of the sentiment "God is on our side."

We took our honeymoon on Rhodes Island. We landed just before Celtic festival of Lughnasadh, supposedly created by the Irish Celtic god Lugh to honour his foster mother. Lugh is a tutelary god for me, and like many other Pagans on a Celtic inspired path, I often call him a sun god. I remember agonising over honouring my own sun god just moments away from the temple of another powerful sun god. I resolved this by performing separate rituals for both gods in the morning sun on our balcony in the countryside, which was an amazing experience.

It's important to note though, that when I refer to Lugh as 'The Celtic Sun God', what I am saying is that Lugh is pretty much as close as the Irish Celts get to having a sun god. There was a Celtic god Belenus, or Bel, but this deity seems not to pop up in Irish mythology, unless one sees Balor, the giant king of the Fomorians, as an etymological link to Bel. Balor had an eye which wreaked damage upon everything it's gaze touched, which could be seen as an aspect of the sun. Lugh himself is not specifically referred to as a personification of the sun, as far as

I am aware, anywhere within source literature. However, there are other references which hint at Lugh's links, metaphorical and otherwise, to the sun, the harvest season, summer and more.

It makes sense that there would not be any clearly defined sun god within Irish Celtic mythology. Foremost, as in many other pantheons, Celtic gods and beings are too convoluted to be tied down to a single aspect. Secondly, once in Ireland after travelling across many countries, the Celts would have noticed that the sun doesn't come out to play quite as much as it does across much of the rest of Europe. So even if there were Celtic tales regarding the sun and its personification, it is likely they were told less than other tales. This means they would have been less likely to have been passed down through oral tradition. We speak of what we know and what is familiar. In a cool and rainy land always in conflict, a dedicated sun god would not have made much as much sense as a god of the crashing sea (Manannán) or a goddess of the blacksmith like Brigid. Lugh, as a master of many trades, adds this feather of "sun god" to his cap. He takes up the task of the solar deity, mostly in the way modern scholars and Pagans re-interpret his tales, and his pivotal role within the ranks of the Tuatha De Danann - the powerful beings who ruled Ireland for so long.

It's very easy for me to get hung up on the Celts and the Greeks, as the former is my ancestral heritage and the latter has been my focus of study for the past decade. However, solar deities appear in many forms all over the world. On the volcanic island of Tenerife, which to the ancients would have seemed to be full of the primal power of fire, they worshiped a deity called Magec. In the ancient Guanche language of the natives, this meant something along the lines of "possessing of radiance". Magec was trapped inside Teide, the island's largest volcano, by the adversary Guayota. Achamán, the creator god of Tenerife, later released Magec. I can only hypothesise, but surely the sun deity bursting out of the top of Mount Teide is the perfect metaphor for the volcano erupting. Yet another way of trying to understand the universe – or indeed, an accurate way of explaining a volcanic eruption, if you look at it from another angle.

Heading east, Amaterasu is a major goddess in Shinto who represents both the sun and the universe. Her names translates to Shining in Heaven, and she was so vital in Japanese mythology that certain chronicles state that all Japanese Emperors are descendants of Amaterasu. Here we see the human link between leadership and the sun. The sun is the centre of our universe to all intents and purposes, and likewise, any leader worth their salt should be too.

In Hopi spirituality and religion, there are many variations in traditions and beliefs. But a common theme is that Tawa is the spirit of the sun, and the creator of all things. Tawa may have made space, and everything in it. Or, Tawa may have instructed a nephew to build nine universes to his design. Either way, to this day it is common for a new-born child to receive a blessing from the sun.

Wherever you go in the world, the sun is always there at some point. In the coldest regions, the sun barely appears during winter, making Winter Solstice rituals where fires are lit to call back the sun even more vital. In the hottest regions, respect is shown to the sun as a giver of life and death, and the fire within the mountain. The constant cycle of the sun's rise and fall we now understand to be about our planet spinning, rather than the sun moving around us. However, that does not take away the vital aspects of these sun gods, many of whom have become an integral part of modern Paganism and spirituality, plus a core part of many living traditions around the globe.

For me, I look up to Lugh on a hot summer's day, and thank him for his many blessings. The Tuatha De Danann were the black cloud that came into Ireland, bringing darkness over the sun for three days and three nights. As I write this, I now witness Lugh, the Tuatha De Danann's own bright light, facing off these new dark clouds in the modern day. Ultimately, he triumphs, and the roofs are resplendent in his glow.

Mabh Savage is a Yorkshire Witch, practicing a nature based craft influenced and inspired by her Celtic Heritage. She is the author of *A Modern Celt*, *Celtic Witchcraft* and *Practically Pagan – An Alternative Guid to Planet Friendly Living*.

Dark Gods

Melusine Draco

In mythology, gods have both positive and negative traits – although there are some whose negativity often gets the better of them. This can be downright evil, dangerous or incredibly destructive and often go well beyond what any seasoned magical practitioner would consider 'acceptable' behaviour. We need, however, to define what we mean by 'dark' – which is not necessarily devilish or demonic – because Dark Gods are common archetypes normally found in fantasy settings. According to the FANDOM subculture, since there were no true gods of evil in mythology, the usual candidates for Dark God status in modern tales are gods of the underworld or pagan deities of considerable fame.

This can be confusing when viewing the older myths as many underworld deities were non-moral; a lot of negative traits of death-gods in the modern mind stems from the way death has become something to fear, while in the past it was considered a natural part of existence. Nevertheless, there is an increasing tendency these days for groups and individuals to portray themselves as being more exciting, adventurous, or more magically adept by covering themselves with a mantle of 'darkness'. Let's make no bones about it – the realm of darkness is an intrinsic part of normal magical practice regardless of path, creed or tradition. In fact, darkness regularly comes to us all as the Earth spins on its axis and another part of the world gets to see the light! Magic used only for good is only singing half the Mass!

Magic *per se* is neither black nor white, good nor evil, and it is often extremely difficult to define exactly what is meant by magic (or magick), as the word has completely different meanings for different people. To some it merely refers to the cabaret act of card tricks and illusion; others think of it in terms of ignorant superstition; while others connect it with the fictional world of *Harry Potter*, or the literary world of *The Lord of the Rings*. For many more, the definition falls between a sinister connection with black masses and dark-doings on one hand, and love potions and healing on the other. An age-old conflict between opposing forces may only have been the by-product of over-active imaginations, but it has always attracted the attention of certain questionable personalities who generally claim to have access to dark powers.

Once we fumble our way past beginner stage, however, we quickly realise that magic is a tantalizing system of opposites: black/white, negative/positive, active/passive, male/female, dark/light, day/night and that the opposite of 'good' isn't necessarily 'evil' – or even lukewarm wicked! And once we reach the path of the Initiate, we find that things haven't changed much, except that we now understand we know *nothing* and have to begin all over again by looking at life, magic and the Universe from a completely different perspective. And we must always remember that in even the deepest esoteric book-learning there are always bits missing! Like that uppermost point that links the human consciousness with the divine, i.e., *Daäth* or Knowledge – the Qabalistic legend of the 'fall' that is a parable of the shutting out of man from Paradise by the destruction of *Daäth* and the establishment of the Abyss. These are the realms that go *beyond* Initiation and which we must still strive towards in order to gain the hidden Wisdom that ultimately leads to Understanding *in* the Darkness.

Nevertheless, there are basic elements of esoteric practice that a colleague of mine always described as '*Ooo-er magic!* meaning that it had been bastardised out of all recognition, and put across as being slightly risqué, or risky, depending on how one viewed the application. The impression is often given by '*Ooo-*

er!' practitioners that certain deities, who are simply Otherworld denizens, or those blessed with an unfavorable physiognomy or unfortunate pedigree, are hailed as the ones to follow. Often accompanied by scorn for those nervous about interacting with such murky energies and, who might be better served taking up macramé.

Who, then, can be described as 'Dark Gods' for the purpose of this essay and who make uneasy companions on the astral? The Greeks, of course, had a name for them: Deimos and Phobos, sons of Ares and Aphrodite. Phobos was the God of Fear and Terror while his brother Deimos was the God of Panic – often accompanying their father into battle. Both were feared and respected by soldiers across the battlefields of Greece because they had particularly cruel personalities, truly reveling in the slaughter and destruction wrought by the perpetually warring armies of Greece and its surrounding neighbours. Phobos was worshipped by warriors before battle in the hope that their opponents would flee the battlefield in fear.

The true personification of the Dark God of fear, however, must surely be Pan. In Greek religion and mythology, Pan ruled over the wilderness and rocky mountain slopes, woodland glades and forests, hunting and rustic music, and a companion of the temperamental nymphs. Yet even the Greeks were hard-pressed to know how to categorise this most ancient of deities who had been revered in his native Arcadia; having no part in the traditional Olympian pantheon because, like other archaic nature spirits, he appears to be much older than the squabbling, fornicating, incestuous tribe that resided atop Mount Olympus.

On his dark side, Pan was said to be the cause of that sudden and groundless panic especially felt by travellers in remote and desolate places. Needless to say, Pan possesses all the conventional abilities of the Olympian gods such as super-human strength and longevity, shape-shifting, stamina and resistance to injury. He also had mystical powers, especially those associated with music and dance, and its magical potency; not to mention a very wily mind, a raucous sense of humour and a voice that instilled terror in the hearer. Like the shepherd he rested at noon, and disliked having his sleep disturbed; Theocritus, the creator of pastoral poetry, gave voice to a well-known Pan-related superstition when he had a goat-herd say: *'In the noontide we may not pipe; 'tis Pan that we fear'* because of the god's rage if woken from his slumber.

If we wish to reconnect with the ancient power of this dark deity in the present then, for all the fear and trepidation Pan can bring, he is easily evoked by those who unconsciously encountered him in wild, remote places – and once contact has been established, he is always there:

I call strong Pan, the substance of the whole,
Etherial, marine, earthly, general soul,
Immortal fire; for all the world is thine,
And all are parts of thee, O pow'r divine.
[The Orphic Hymns]

Primordial gods of chaos are perfect contenders for the appellation 'Dark Gods' because their cosmologies are hidden in the mists of time. In Greek mythology, Chaos was the beginning of all things. The word means chasm, emptiness, and vast void in Greek; in the creation myths, it is the primordial or formless state created by the separation of heaven and earth and viewed as the lower atmosphere surrounding earth. Erebus was one of these primordial deities, born out of the primeval void where Chaos was considered to be the personification of the deep darkness and shadow.

The title of 'Grand Master of Darkness', however, must surely go to Set – a god of deserts, storms, disorder, violence and chaos in the ancient Egyptian religion. He is sometimes depicted as a red-haired dog-like beast with a forked tail and truncated ears, known as a sha (or, to modern-day scholars, as the Set-Animal). In the Early Dynastic Period he was the deity who saved Re from the serpent Apophis, an evil creature who tried to stop the sun god's journey through the night sky toward dawn. In doing so, Set assured that the sun would rise the next morning.

By the New Kingdom, however, he was known as the murderer of his brother Osiris in order to reign over the world, and then tried to murder his nephew, Horus. From the New Kingdom onward, after monumental religious upheavals, Set was regarded as a villain (with different variations) but it was not always so. The oldest *Pyramid Texts* present us with compelling evidence that Horus and Set originally had nothing to do with Osiris, and that Osiris does not figure greatly in the earlier Utterances. The conflict between Horus and Set is the older version of what later became known as the Osirian myth.

Yet there is an even earlier strata of belief where Set alone provided the guidance for the dead ruler's soul into the afterlife. We catch glimpses of this earliest belief in concepts that were carried over into Dynastic times and found in one of Set's titles, 'Son of Nut'. Set is so frequently and readily referred to in this way that this designation alone is enough to identify him. In the primeval belief, Nut was the destination of the king's soul, the Imperishable Stars. The Dynastic Nut was the personification of the starry heavens; Set was the Deep Space beyond.

Once the Osirian-cult gained the ascendancy and the deceased king became fully identified with Osiris, the Horus-Set *psychopompi* were dispensed with Horus the Elder becoming Horus the Child, and the older tale of the feud between Horus and Set adapted wholesale into the new religion to fit the needs of the Osirian-cultus.

Nevertheless, Set was also possessed of a quality that the Egyptians could not dismiss so easily: his tremendous strength and courage, and his ability to defend his fellow *neteru* against forces greater than themselves. Setian energies are those of yesterday and those of tomorrow – and, for many, will not sit comfortably with the passivity of today's pagan thought. Then, as now, Set's qualities were those of the individual as opposed to society *per se* – the expression of individual Will going against a society that held *Ma'at* (order and harmony) as sacrosanct. For Set is not a god-form to be bullied, negotiated with or demanded from: and his title – 'Son of Nut' – suggests that she should be used as the balancing power during magical working. By day or night, Nut is the space that hinted at all concealed from view since her 'body' represented the limits of the domain Re travelled through each day. 'Our Lady of the Starry Heavens' as Crowley referred to her, did not represent the whole of existing space – that is Set's domain. The following text is, of course, pure Setian and includes words that can be used as a magical invocation to this ancient god of cosmic forces:

> *Brother, As long as you burn you belong to life.*
> *You say you want ME with you in the Beyond!*
> *Forget the Beyond!*
> *When you bring your flesh to rest*
> *And thus reach the Beyond,*
> *In that stillness shall I alight upon you;*
> *Thus united we shall form the Abode.*
> *For above is exalted by below*

From a magical perspective, we need to look at Setian imagery in a constructive way. To invoke the power of Set for ordinary, mundane magical workings would be like taking a sledge-hammer to crack a nut! Geraldine Pinch writing in *Magic in Ancient Egypt,* explains that Set was the force of chaos that should be invoked to fight like with like. "When something dangerous and chaotic has to be overcome, a being possessing those qualities needed to be enlisted on your side," she observed. Therefore, Set is called upon as a guide and protector from the cosmic darkness and all that it conceals, i.e., ignorance, hypocrisy and superstition; he is the Path to hidden knowledge, wisdom and understanding. It is only in his negative form that he represents confusion and social/cosmic disorder. On a magical and mystical level, Set is much more important and brings to mind those lines from Aleister Crowley's *Book of the Law*, written thousands of years later, where Hadit (Set) refers to his 'secondary' place, hidden behind Nuit:

> *In the sphere I am everywhere the centre, as she, the circumference, is nowhere found. Yet she shall be known & I never ... I am the flame that burns in every heart of man, and in the core of every star. I am Life, and the giver of Life, yet therefore is the knowledge of me the knowledge of death.*

For contemporary Companions of Set, the focus of their devotions aims to re-connect with that Old Order; those primordial energies that have their source in *zep tepi*, the 'First Time' and the cosmic creation. Magically speaking, these are not favours or influences that can be bartered for – more like taking advantage of a gigantic wave of energy that can add impetus to a working – rather than petitioning for divine intervention. With Setian magic there has never been a truer adage than 'Be careful what you ask for', because misplaced channeling can bring through those dynamic, uncontrollable energies for which Set is famous. You may ask for a divine spark to ignite a candle and finish up incinerating your life – because misplaced Setian energy *is* radioactive destruction on a cosmic scale!

Billie Walker-John wrote to her co-author Alan Richardson (*The Inner Guide to Egypt*):

> "I like your ideas about 'Dark Magic' but I don't want to frighten anyone off and have them thinking we're dishing up 'black' magic, yet at the same time we need to be clear that

working with Set is not something for the eager, innocent neophytes either. It *IS* 'Dark Magic' without any of the negative connotations associated with 'black' magic. It's no easy ride, we both know that."

Added to this, a good rummage around in the 'darker' aspects of the monotheistic religions is always good for a bit of *'Ooo-er magic!'* providing those they are trying to impress haven't bothered too much with conducting any research into the background claims of the participants, or their 'occult tradition'. Where would we be, for instance, without the supporting demonic cast of the Book of Revelation, the Apocrypha and Pseudepigrapha? Like sexual orientations, a person's magical inclinations are just that: *personal.* They are governed by an individual's own ethics and morality in what my tutor always described as forty shades of grey (long before *that* book came out). My Welsh slate grey, for instance, might be your deepest black; your pewter grey might be my Arctic white – again, it's all a matter of individual perception.

All seasoned magical practitioners learn to walk safely on the dark side they occasionally need to tread but they do it with a certain amount of fear and a lot of respect. Because as that same colleague often commented: *'If you don't feel the fear, you ain't doing it right!'* So, the next time you see an online promotion trawling for those who want to learn the 'real' hidden secrets of magic from those who walk on the dark side with some shady entity, and which reads as though it's come straight from J R R Tolkien (but less literary) … it probably has!

Melusine Draco originally trained in the magical arts of traditional British Old Craft with Bob and Mériém Clay-Egerton. She has been a magical and spiritual instructor for over 20 years with Arcanum and the Temple of Khem, and is the writer of numerous popular books.

Warriors Gods

Dorothy Abrams

The attributes of war are divided among warrior Gods. There are hundreds of them across cultures. Some stand in the midst of battle to protect their champions. They accompany soldiers at the perimeter standing guard or scouting adversaries. They guard the gates of home and the loved ones left behind. They send chaos into the enemy before the battle engages. They may love, safeguard, trick or shield their people. They may care for widows and orphans of war or they may conduct the fallen through the gates of death to the other side. They are strategic planners. They are impetuous fighters. Theirs is a long view, a wide perspective that extends beyond local politics and personal quarrels. They regard the rise and fall of nations in war, the loss of cultures, languages or wisdom from a city laid flat by attack. They see the sense and justice of war in a world which has yet to value peace. The Warrior Gods reflect traits ranging from belligerent enemies in combat to sacrificial heroes saving or protecting the vulnerable. Sometimes someone's worst night mare is another's shining light. Destruction or rescue. Fearsome or heroic. These may be the faces of the same warrior. How we relate to the Warrior Gods depends on our view of their mission.

But what is their mission? Are the Gods interested in protecting their people? Do they engage with human history to defend their heroes? Are they amused by our politics and goad us on to play out the battles emerging from our fears or greed? Do they take sides? Are we pawns in their disputes? Likely the answer is all of the above depending on the geography, times and the Gods.

I find stories about the Warrior Gods difficult more often than inspiring. I like to think we have evolved beyond egocentric consciousness and with us so do the Gods of war. Surely after millennia of experience they know better. Then I consider current events and know human or divine, we have learned very little. We remain caught up in the same kind of conflicts as we always were: revenge for the loss of face, punishment for acts of aggression or control of land, natural resources or shipping lanes. Armies rise from failed diplomacy claiming they protect vulnerable populations, that they defend hearth, home and freedom. Behind those missions are the secret motivations creating war: the power of the military industrial complex, investment and profit; weapons testing; strategic war games gone live in real time to act out military tactics. Do the Gods care about such things? Perhaps they have the same or other secrets. Their concerns are not frozen in antiquity. If they play a chess game with nations then they are equally entrenched in modern warfare on the board game of history.

Yet Warrior Gods have interests beyond battle and victory. They have objectives in nation building and reconstruction. They are historians, poets and story tellers. Some are magicians. Others are sacrificial heroes. Some are lovers, husbands and parents. Some are belligerent hotheads.

Ares carries that latter reputation. He is known as quick to pick up an offense. He is quicker yet to offend. He had no hesitation in seducing Aphrodite, his brother's wife. The couple was humiliated by the wronged husband Hephaestus with a bronze net trap and left ensnared for the Gods to mock. Nevertheless, Ares and Aphrodite birthed Harmonia and Eros, clearly their mother's children. He also fathered Fear, Terror and Strife with whom he most often dwelt.

Ares is criticized for changing sides in battle during the Trojan war against his father's command. He is defeated by the armies led by his sister Athena. Wounded, he appealed to his father and received little sympathy. Ares is scorned for his losses and poor judgment by many of the Greek city states.

Sparta, a military stronghold, is the exception. A rare temple is dedicated solely to Ares in Sparta despite Zeus' assessment of his son as the least of the Gods. The Greeks did not like Ares but found him necessary.

By contrast Mars who is often cited as the Roman equivalent of Ares is counted by his people as second only to his father Jupiter. Mars is celebrated throughout the Empire as patron of the Legions and source of their disciplined success. Where Ares fights emotionally, expecting his strength to prevail, Mars is a military strategist. He uses plans, troop movements and sound training to bring victory home to Rome.

Like Ares, however, Mars is a fool for love and by our standards equally dishonorable. Mars woos Rome's Goddess of Love, Venus and suffers a similar entrapment as Ares. They have children of the same names. However, Mars woos Minerva, the wisdom/Warrior Goddess, whereas Ares fights with Athena his sister known for wisdom and war strategy, most famously in the Peloponnesian War in 431 BCE. Mars was unsuccessful in his campaign to win over Minerva, the virgin Goddess. He engaged an older Goddess, Anna Perenna, Goddess of Time, to intercede with Minerva. Anna appreciated the handsome God and agreed to help in order to win him for herself. She disguised herself as Minerva and tricked Mars into marriage. The ruse did result in mockery but seems not to have diminished Mars standing with the Gods and celebrants. Nevertheless, Anna's March festival is known for its bawdy humor and sexuality so perhaps the mockery was directed at her.

Mars was originally an agricultural God. The relationship with the land and war strikes at early defensive actions to secure territory and sustenance. An army of farmers is not our first understanding of the military in the 21st century. That may be because so few people are farmers these days. We war over territory related to natural resources and traditional boundaries. In a time when boundaries were more fluid, fields and grazing ranges were more clearly defined. The agricultural war Gods rose to defend their holdings. Their connection to the land was grit under the farmers' fingernails.

In that sense, it was not unusual to find an agricultural God surveying his territory. Early on in his history Mars came upon Rhea Silvia asleep in the forest. Because of her beauty he deepened her sleep and proceeded to impregnate her with the twins Romulus and Remus. When her pregnancy was revealed she was judged and the boys were ordered drowned. However, they ended up in the wilderness on dry land, subsequently raised by a she-wolf and fed by a woodpecker. Since that bird is a symbol of Mars it might be that he cared for his sons. In any case they are the founders of Rome which adds to Mars' positive reputation despite his rape of their mother. Times change. Mars heroic stature is blemished in the #MeToo era. Male warriors of Rome felt no such judgements.

In short both Ares and Mars are battle Gods. Ares enjoys the battle for the blood lust leaving strategy to his sister. Mars is more thoughtful on how to prevail in the clash or armies but never shrinks from the carnage necessary to win.

Tyr of the Norsemen is known for individual conflicts, though warriors are encouraged to call on him for victory in war. Not many of his stories have survived the ages. He is an ancient deity. He is counted as a hero-warrior particularly for the sacrifice of his hand (arm) to the giant wolf Fenir. By placing his hand in the wolf's mouth, he distracted Fenir so the other warriors could bind him. Tyr had cared for Fenir as a pup and acted to restrain him to prevent his rampages through the population. He could not allow the destruction wrought by the wolf to continue so sacrificed a friendship as well as a limb. The wolf remains imprisoned until the last days of the Death of the Gods (Ragnarok). When released he will destroy Tyr and others as a new world is made with new Gods.

Tyr's loss of a limb is not an uncommon sacrifice for men

returning from war, if they return at all. The heroism of the soldier is often shrugged off as part of the job. It is a loss they live with, in Tyr's case for the millennia. Tyr earned his place as guardian of oaths, God of treaties and justice. His was a champion of the formalities of war similar to the Geneva Conventions and the International Humanitarian Law. It is these rules and the influence of Tyr that prevents us from descending into Mar's chaos and Ares' bloodthirst. Tyr is an essential Warrior God if we are to avoid barbarism. Tyr is a warrior but he is also fair. Known as a law giver he balances strength and bravery with justice.

Other aspects of war in the Norse lands belong to Thor and Odin. Like Ares, Thor is a fierce fighter, unafraid of gore. He champions the battle frenzy needed to win. Odin by contrast presents the psychological nature of the warrior and defender of heroes. Along with that he is a great magician that can turn the tide of battle. He is a poet who can relate the stories of victory and sacrifice. Warrior Gods divide the various aspects of war among themselves, so that no single God holds all the cards. In this we see the great complexity of the divine Warriors.

This division of power is true also in Egypt. Egyptian Warrior Gods include Horus, God of war and protection. He is a sky God so now he might also be the patron of the air force. Montu is a God of war and valor. Set is a dark God associated with war, death, and battle with his own siblings. He resides in the deserts and creates storms. One might make a stretch and call on him in the Middle East wars of the 1990's and continuing. One assault in this series of campaigns was called Desert Storm. Wepwawet appears as wolf-God of war and death. His aspects eventually merged with Anubis, God of death and the afterlife.

The Egyptian crocodile God Sobek demonstrates how a warrior combines attributes of war even though others of the pantheon hold claim to them. As a crocodile, Sobek demonstrates chaotic war representing stealth, strength and raw power. The crocodile is submerged and strikes grabbing its prey. He holds it tight in his jaws as it twists and turns to escape before he drowns it. Sobek is patron of the military and leads them to victory. He is allied with death because there is no victory without casualties. He is also a healer, fertility God and creator. During various periods of Egyptian history, he is combined with Ra and Horus the Elder as a solar deity crossing the heavens. Sobek, like the crocodile of the Nile, is ferocious in his protection of the Pharaoh, particularly from evil magic. He defended those who were at risk along the Nile, principally from attack by reptilian crocodiles.

Sobek is primeval in his sexuality. He takes women from their husbands. He is praised for his assault of women. He is violent and virile as is the crocodile. His wife is the Snake Goddess Renenutet, continuing the reptile family tree. However, their son was Khonsu the Moon God who gambles with Thoth as champion of Nut. Renenutet brought luck and assets to the ancient Egyptians, both necessary for victorious armies.

Elsewhere in Africa, Ogun is one of the Warrior Gods among the Orishas of west Africa. He is credited with making the way on earth for the other Orishas. As a warrior he is God of weapons and tools and he heals. He is a champion of justice who seeks revenge on liars and frauds. He rides into battle on a white horse; uses magic in battle and his protection of the vulnerable among his followers. Like so many Warrior Gods, he loves women and especially the Goddess of love and beauty, Erzulie. He is part of the African diaspora and is worshipped wherever Voudoo and Santeria rituals flourish. He is hero of the Haitian civil war, favoring red clothing and cigars. People call on him for intervention with official persecution from rogue governments and animosity from personal enemies.

What is our connection to these Warrior Gods in the 21st century? Soldiers on patrol amid IEDs or snipers might do well to seek a patron among them, advisably from one's own ethnicity or spiritual practice. Asking for protection on patrol is clearly within the purview of certain deities. Warriors perhaps understand the need more than gentler Gods. If one goes into battle on the field or in street fighting house to house the same patron may accompany his warrior. Wounded warriors can call on healer warrior Gods for restored health. Officers leading their units or commanders sending out tactical orders may call on the strategists for wisdom and success. If people at home have family members and friends at war, then intercession from the Gods to bring them home safely is both a comfort and effective intervention.

We should not wait until we receive marching orders to make connection with the Warrior Gods. Before signing up, research the history and character of the God as well as the appropriate rituals, altars or requests is wise. Make it clear in these times blood sacrifice is not an option. Know what is welcomed by one God may be an offense to another. Understand the consequences of your liaison. Asking Ares for victory might create a bloody disaster or victory, but not likely a clean military operation. The unit might win and be caught up in charges of war crimes. Calling on Tyr for victory might involve sacrifices one did not intend. Calling on Sobek might blind reason but defend the cause perhaps with a magical outcome.

In our military campaigns we see a faint hand of the Warrior Gods at work. Ritual and meditation to better understand that working and the magic that may attend their presence is an interesting and wise practice, even for civilians. Was Set really present in Gulf Wars code named Desert Shield and Desert Storm? Or is he limited to the Egyptian lands and Arab Spring? Can we find a resolution to the tensions in that part of the world without turning the sands and rivers to blood? Perhaps Tyr can answer that. Or is he limited to the European terrorist assaults and challenges of the right wing nationalist terror? Will Ogun remove liars from our politics and protect the world from their deceit? Or is he a God of his own people from the African diaspora? We do not know the answers to these questions from common literature and popular ritual practice. A great deal of psychic and ceremonial work awaits us if we would campaign with the War Gods and they champion us. Proceeding with them requires great skill and magic. It is not taken on lightly. It might, however, save the world just now.

Dorothy Abrams, a Central New York feminist Witch, is co-founder of the Web PATH Center and author of *Identity and the Quartered Circle; Studies in Applied Wicca.*

Planetary Gods

Scott Irvine

It is the same interaction of the planets that create the conditions we find affecting our planet today as it was for the people of the first cities of Sumer around 6,000 years ago. Our beautiful world is sandwiched between Venus, the goddess of love on our sun side and the god of war Mars, protecting us from dangers coming in from the outer solar system. Inside the orbit of Venus and closest planet to the Sun is Mercury, the messenger of the gods who, despite his small size, helps significantly in the influence the gods had over humanity. Beyond Mars is the mighty gas giant Jupiter the king of gods who ensures that justice prevails across the universe. Our furthermost planet and extent of the known universe at the time was Saturn, the ringed planet and god of boundaries and limits, standing guard protecting us from the dangers of the rest of the universe.

Orbiting earth is our Moon, its gravitational forces stirring up the seas and its powerful energies throughout its waxing and waning cycle affecting everyone. Despite being known today as the feminine energy of the goddess, the Moon's early incarnation is the powerful male energy of a god, a god that ruled over all the other planetary gods before he became a she and rapidly demoted through the ranks.

While Asia was building cities in the desert out of mud bricks, the New Stone Age Europeans were erecting great stone circles and temples to record the movements of the sun and moon and a newly discovered planet we know as Venus that reappears in the morning and evening skies after a twenty day absence during her transit behind the sun heralding in the beginning of spring in the northern hemisphere. The Sumerians built pyramids called ziggurats, temples that were placed at the centre of each city to honour a planetary deity or elemental god that controlled the weather. At the heart of their beliefs was the trinity of forces they saw as the Father, the Son and the primeval feminine force of the 'holy' spirit and wife of God. Father was the Moon god Nanna, his son Utu the Sun god and his daughter the divine spirit, the fertility goddess of love of life, Inanna, the Queen of Venus.

The God of heaven is An, the ruler of the universe and everything in it. His union with the earth goddess Ki gives birth to nature and with his half-sister and wife Antu, the Air God Enlil is born to manage things on earth. Air gives breath to nature and brings storms to refresh and renew the old. Despite being the royal heir to his father's throne, Enlil is usurped by his step brother Enki, the water god, who controls the rain that floods the rivers, of Mesopotamia each spring bringing fertility to the parched desert.

The Sumerian way of life changed forever around 2,300BCE when a powerful army from Akkad swept down from the north on chariots, wearing bronze armour and helmets to conquer the region between the rivers of Euphrates and Tigris. They were led by Sargon the Great who made Babylon his central powerbase from which he governed Mesopotamia. The Babylonian priests were aware of four new planets that crossed the heavens alongside the Sun, Moon and Venus; Mars, Saturn, Jupiter and Mercury. The trinity of the father, the Moon God Sin, the son, Sun God Shamash and the sacred spirit of Ishtar and Ereshkigal, the light and dark (morning and evening) aspects of Venus, oversee the planetary pantheon of Nergal the god of Mars, Ninurta the god of Saturn, Marduk the god of Jupiter and Nabu the god of Mercury.

The Moon god Sin is the offspring of the air god Enlil and the grain goddess Ninlil. By having the strongest visible effect over the earth's tidal waters and creative human minds, Sin became the chief god of the early Babylonian hierarchy known as the Anunnaki which means 'from heaven to earth came'. The other gods consult him for his wisdom at his temple in the old capital state of Ur. He is the father of the other two in the trinity, Shamash and Ishtar.

The Moon god nourishes the cattle by raising the marsh waters each spring ensuring the growth of the grass the herds rely on to bring prosperity and fertility to the city farms. Each evening, Sin rides his crescent shaped boat called the 'Shining Boat of Heaven' and sails it across the night sky. Each spring, the king of Ur assumes the identity of Sin and enacts the sacred fertility marriage with the high priestess chosen from the royal family to play the earth goddess. Sin loses his position as the chief of the gods when his cousin Marduk defeats the Mother Goddess in single combat gaining control of her 'Tablets of Destiny' becoming King of the gods, Master of the Universe and leader of the most powerful force on earth, demoting Sin to a general in his army.

The son of Sin is the wise Sun god Shamash, to whom kings and subjects alike would pray for help in their daily lives, be it for an heir to the throne or food for the mouth of a starving newborn baby. Shamash sits in judgement over the actions of both gods and men and being made of light could see all things, both good and wicked enabling him to see into the future.

Each morning the scorpion men opens a gate in the vast mountain of Mashu allowing Shamash into the sky were he rides his chariot of fire towards another great mountain in the west where he disappears into the depths of the earth until he reaches the eastern gate once more. The Sun was the only god to have crossed underneath the mountains of Mashu and the waters of death to discover the secrets of immortality that he reserves for the gods alone.

The Babylonian king Hammurabi who ruled the Babylonian empire 1792-1750BCE received from Shamash a collection of laws called the 'Code of Hammurabi' that set prices, wages and a fair tax system encouraging support for both god and king.

The god of Mars is Nergal, the son of Ninhursag, the 'fertile Lady of the stony ground' and her husband the Water god and Lord of the Earth, Enki. The god of war refuses to stand on ceremony when an ambassador for the Queen of the underworld arrives in her place at a great feast for the gods and goddesses. His actions angers Ereshkigal who asks for his life which was quickly granted; nobody refuses the queen of death, but Nergal was not ready to join the ranks of her abode. When he journeys to the underworld, he takes fourteen of his best men to capture, control and guard each of the seven gates into hell for his return. Once inside Ereshkigal's palace he slaughters the ambassador before coming face to face with the goddess of darkness. For once, the lethal evil eye of death fails Ereshkigal and Nergal seizes his chance, dragging her to the ground ready to cut off her head, when she offers him marriage and the kingdom of the underworld. Nergal accepts her offer, dries her tears and made love with her for six days. It is Nergal who escorts the souls of the dead into the subterranean world of ghosts and allows those to escape when requested by his superiors.

Nergal leads the gods into battle against the demons that constantly threaten humanity. He fights alongside his half-brother Ninurta, the god of Saturn and guardian of the solar system. Ninurta is the thunderstorm god with his heavy rain flooding the parched land during the spring floods of the Euphrates and Tigris rivers. He shared his mother with Nergal but his father was the sky god Enlil, Enki's half-brother. In battle, Ninurta was a lion headed eagle destroying everything in his path. His aggression causes nature and some of the elements to rebel against him. Victorious, Ninurta punishes nature to be at the mercy of humanity and the elements that supported him are rewarded to become much sought after precious treasures. When Ninurta returned ecstatic from a battle once, he was loud and excited, recounting his heroism to his mother while putting away his weapons and stabling his horses. The noise and commotion causes a row between Ninurta and the quiet loving Enlil which threatened to get out of control. It would have ended in all-out war if it was not for the quick thinking of Ninurta's barber shoving his master away with the promise of a grand new haircut.

The Babylonian chief of all the gods and king of the planet Jupiter, Marduk is credited for creating universal order from the primeval chaos that went before. On earth, Marduk is the god of justice and first born son of Enki and a serpent goddess. He used his guile to rise up through the ranks of the Anunnaki order of gods, from a local fertility god to the ruler of the whole planet in a very short time, gradually gaining authority over the moon, rain, justice, wisdom and war. Before meeting the aging Stone Age mother goddess Tiamat, the 'Lady of Life' in battle, Marduk is elected as king and champion of the Anunnaki if he could defeat the advancing army of demons led by the 'She Devil' Tiamat herself. Kill Tiamat and Marduk would possess the magical 'Tablets of Destiny' that had belonged to the mother goddess since the beginning of space and time. Having disposed of the evil demon goddess, his great, great great grandmother incidentally, he takes the magical tablets from her chest and fixes them to his own. The universe belonged to him. As king, Marduk establishes his own rule on earth introducing the concept of an advancing progression of time and personal wealth and power. He bases the calendar on the phases of the Sun rather than the cycles of the Moon, creates the constellations in the heavens and gives birth to the tame beasts that were once the savage human.

Marduk was the first royal Anunnaki to take a human woman as a wife and queen. Marrying Sarpanit made it a common practice between the other gods and humanity. Marduk and his human queen give birth to Nabu, the god of Mercury, who became a Babylonian priest king and intermediary between humanity and god; the mediator between master and pupil.

Meanwhile the climate of earth was warming up as the last ice age continued to retreat further north, opening up the lush fertile forests of Europe becoming popular to the Asian consciousness, giving rise to the developing Greek and Roman empires. The planetary gods needed to be reinvented and improved for the European market.

The Moon god Sin becomes the virgin huntress of the forest Artemis for the rising Greek empire around 700BCE. The goddess is the twin sister of the Sun god Apollo from the union of Zeus and the Titan Leto. Artemis is a goddess with attitude and a powerful force to be reckoned with. The Romans called her Diana.

Two gods are associated with the Sun, the Titan Helios, seen as the orb of the star itself and Apollo the solar light. Helios rides his golden chariot drawn by four horses from his eastern palace to his western palace throughout the day, returning home on the river Oceanus during the night. Sometimes Apollo joins Helios in his own chariot pulled by lions, armed with his bow and arrow hunting humans to inflame with creativity; he is the celestial archer whose arrows never miss its target. The god of light performs many great feats growing up, once slaying the earth serpent Python at Delphi where he had an oracle revealing people's fate to them. Apollo is associated with music and poetry, medicine and prophecy and protects cattle and sheep. He loved handsome men as well as beautiful women, nymphs and goddesses. The Romans knew him as Sol. In Egypt the Sun god Ra ruled supreme.

The Babylonian goddess of love becomes the Greek goddess of love and beauty Aphrodite, another offspring of Zeus. The goddess loves to weave plots tempting the gods to fall in love with mortals. She is always upsetting someone and generally pays the price one way or another. She has to share her true love Adonis with her sister Persephone, the queen of death; a kind of fertility triangle reflecting life, death and the rebirth of nature.

Nergal becomes the handsome Ares, god of war and only son of Zeus with his wife Hera. The Greeks fear him, afraid of his great pleasure in violence and cruelty. He had four children with Aphrodite, the twin boys Phobos (panic), Deimos (fear) and daughters Eris (strife) and sweet Harmonia. Ares instigates violence for its own sake making a very unstable god to work with. He is uncontrolled passion and the original bad boy. The Roman Mars is a much less aggressive god who was popular with the Roman army.

Ninurta is known as the Titan Cronus, god of time and father of Zeus. He becomes the king of the giants after castrating his father Uranus, the sky, while making love to his mother Gaia, the earth, separating the pair forever. Fearing his offspring would do the same with him, Cronus ate them all at birth except Zeus who made his father spew up his brothers and sisters. After a great battle with the Titans, the Olympians rule supreme over the earth and exile the older gods to the underworld leaving the way open for the Roman Saturn to replace Cronus.

The Babylonian king of the universe became the father of the gods, Zeus who had a hand in everything the Olympians got up to. With his thunderbolt he kept order over the world. Zeus had his pick of goddesses, nymphs and women, fathering thousands of children. A Phoenician princess called Europa is abducted by Zeus disguised as a bull taking her from Asia across the Mediterranean into Europe, named after her, settling on the beautiful Greek island of Crete. Zeus becomes the Roman god of justice, Jupiter.

Nabu, the son of Marduk becomes Hermes the son of Zeus whose mother was the nature nymph Maia. Hermes is the messenger of the gods mediating between Zeus and humanity. He invented the Lyre by stretching string across a tortoise shell that he offered to Apollo for stealing his sheep. Hermes even stole the sun god's bow and arrows but Zeus made him return them. Hermes is the patron of thieves and travellers and blessed with the gift of articulation. When he is not deceiving or stealing from the other gods, Hermes helps to deliver the dead souls to the underworld. The Romans knew him as Mercury, the god of trade and commerce who was associated with speed and communication.

As the planets spiral through space and time, dancing and singing they constantly change the conditions in the solar system as it journeys into the future around the outer reaches of our galaxy.

Scott Irvine has followed the path of the goddess for over a decade. He is the author of *Ishtar and Ereshkigal*.

Sleeping Gods

Philip Kane

A few years ago, the author Neil Gaiman wrote a novel titled American Gods. More recently, the novel has been adapted as a television series. As is usually the case, the book is superior to the televised version, but both are worthy of attention. One of the underlying premises of American Gods is an old one, but cleverly recycled. That is, the gods in Gaiman's fictional world rely on the accumulated energy of worshippers for their very existence. The more worshippers they have, the stronger the god; no worshippers, and the god will fade away. The plot is much more complex than merely that, of course, but for the present purposes of this essay it's the aspect that is particularly relevant.

In Gaiman's story, Mr Wednesday – aka Woden/Odin – assembles a motley band of forgotten gods to battle against the newly created gods of the internet age, and to restore their ancient status. There is a struggle between the old and the new. The old gods have no wish to be forgotten. Fiction often manages to register and express truths more effectively than documentary. In our own, historical, past our ancestors lived in a world that was teeming with gods. Deities lived as immanent powers in rivers and ponds, in forests and in pastures, in living creatures. They were integral to the breathing, natural world, as much a part of everyday life and nature as the crops and the flocks and the hearthfire. They were neighbours rather than overseers, and the healthy relationship of people with their gods and goddesses was essential to the wellbeing of the community.

At the same time, not unlike human neighbours, such gods were often localised, gods of this hearth or that specific woodland, or gods of the particular clan or tribe. These are gods that the modern world has largely forgotten; gods that have fallen asleep, neglected and often nameless as humanity bustles on around them.

There has been a substantial body of work made publicly available on the search for forgotten or lost goddesses – see, for instance, Finding Elen (edited by Caroline Wise) and Searching for Sulis by Alan Richardson and Margaret Haffenden. There is rather less on our forgotten gods, although there are exceptions – Bladud and perhaps others appear briefly in that book on Sulis, and the work of John and Caitlin Matthews regarding the Mabon also springs to mind. It's understandable that in a society that remains fundamentally patriarchal, the recovery of lost and forgotten goddesses will take a degree of precedence as the effort goes on to revive and revitalise the place of the divine feminine. But the balance of polarity, the heart of magic, requires both sides of the divine equation to be fulfilled. Where are our forgotten Gods?

One answer, obviously enough, is, "Where they have always been". The monotheistic religions – and most specifically Christianity, in the context of Europe – have turned our wild gods into demons and imps, malevolent spirits to haunt the dark hours and terrify the ill-educated. Industrialisation has overlaid their earth with concrete and brick, with tarmac and iron, laced it with toxic chemicals and plastic waste. Yet the gods have still not been uprooted from the soil or from the remains of ancient woodland, or from the hearts of humans who still hear the whisper of their lost names on the wind.

The search to recover them and to restore them to a rightful place in the modern world may be considered a form of poetic quest, if we pause to consider that term poetic in its broadest and fullest sense. In other words, it's a quest based on analogy and on the non-rational, rather than upon the rational and the intellectual; and the quarry (for want of a better term) can be elusive, sometimes even reluctant to be found.

Where we might begin is in the naming of things. Some of the old gods have left such traces in the landscape and even in the hubbub of our urban centres. Look at the names of certain woods and hills, even some street names. The rare ones may retain a connection to a god in that way, albeit weathered by the passing of time and the fading of memory. It's to be noted, here, that many ancient gods were generally known by the naming of their functions, rather than by true personal names. Cernunnos, for example, approximately translates as simply "the horned one". He may be among the best known of horned gods, but is by no means the only one. Local gods may be subsumed, by name, into such grander figures. Herne's Wood is not necessarily related specifically to Herne himself, for instance, but could be connected to a more localised deity, perhaps even of that particular place. This is the sort of thing that will require deeper research, and development of a relationship with the specific site.

Again, saint names are fairly commonplace. While the adaptation of ancient goddesses into female saints is a well-known phenomenon (Brigid being among the most obvious), the same process absorbed various Pagan gods into a Christian worldview. They were mostly gods known by Roman names by then, as long beforehand the Roman Empire had already absorbed older, native gods into their own official pantheon, for instance associating Cernunnos with Mercury and so on. It can be necessary to dig a little deeper to find the god behind the curtain.

As a further note, given that Christianity condemned the old gods by conscripting them into the legions of Hell, places that are said to have connections to the Devil, to demons, imps and the like may also present a clue to the presence of older deities. There may also be traces to be found in local folklore, in stories and songs associated with particular places.

All of this constitutes merely the preliminaries. We need

to build a relationship with our forgotten, ancestral gods and that demands direct contact, above and beyond any literary investigation. Most are, frankly, so deeply buried by the accumulation of time and culture and technology that they have left no visible trace whatsoever. Yet they can still be found.

One of the keys to this is simply in the sense of presence that we may experience in a certain location. And that can only be accessed through our living familiarity with the places that our forgotten gods inhabit. We need to remake our living relationship with the wild. We have to go back into the woods and the wildernesses, whatever is left of them, where gods will speak to us on the wind and in the rustling of the leaves, in birdsong and the imperceptible stirrings of the earth. More than this, though. For there is no part of this Earth that is not sacred, and all of it is animated by the Divine.

I live in an urban centre, my house on a busy main arterial road a fifteen-minute walk from the central shopping area. It's low on the slopes of a deep valley leading down to the broad river that the town leans against. A tributary once ran down the valley and along a street still named The Brook to join its big sister. Any sign of it is long gone. In its place, on the valley floor, there's a narrow alleyway lined with garages and discarded mattresses. At one point in its course, even after it had been buried under concrete and asphalt, where it had originally curled around a spur in the landscape it still rose up as a source for a public bath house and an ornamental fountain, but even they have vanished, victims of the urban planners and their visions for a bright new future. Yet summoning the nerve to walk that sad alleyway, pacing out the grey path that was once a living river, I can still sense the current of energy beneath my feet. And within that current, distant yet still discernible, there may be heard the voice of a goddess whispering across aching centuries of neglect.

The same sort of process can help us to rediscover the

forgotten male deities. Walk the paths through remnants of ancient woodland. Meditate at sacred sites, at hill forts, in forest and on moorland, in caves and groves. Listen for their voices, whispering in the leaves or on the wind. Watch for them in pathworkings and on vision quests. Call to them from your Circles and Temples. Pay close attention to your dreams.

How though to bring back a lost god, once found, more fully into the consciousness of the world? In a time when the gods that most people worship are speed, and consumerism, and celebrity – the shallow deities of a dispirited age – the work is both difficult and essential. Difficult because we have few if any clues as to who or what the lost gods are. What may wake and summon them? What ritual, what understanding, has been lost? Essential because the Land is dying – more accurately, being killed – by the gathering layers of concrete, by poisons in the soil and in the air; by the rage and hatred and greed of humans who have forgotten that the Land and life are sacred, and right relationship with the sacred is essential to our very humanity. Rediscovering and reconnecting with our forgotten gods is a necessary act of ecology when so much of the natural world is being extinguished.

And reconnection is a process. Gods, even those whose names and purposes have been obscured by time and invasion and industry, need sustenance too. If we merely act by being in their places of power with an open heart, and some small offering – a flower, a ribbon, a song – they will hear. They will come back to us if we call to them gently, in a spirit of true service rather than in some imagined domination over them.

At this point I must also sound a warning. The harsh truth is that some ancient gods may have been forgotten for good reasons. What place is there in our modern world for some archaic and belligerent war god who demands that his place of worship should be festooned with the decapitated heads of fallen warriors? Whatever we may think of his past, it is difficult to see how he can fit into our present and our future. Some such gods may be adaptable to our age. Some will not be. This is where discrimination is needed. Looking again at our hypothetical war god, can he perhaps be persuaded that his role now is to act as a power within campaigns for social justice? And can he be satisfied with a more appropriate form of trophy than heads?!

This is not uncommon with the forgotten gods. The fact is that many male deities are gods of the hunt, of battle, of thunder and storm. Gods of strong, often fierce, primeval forces. And they are frequently, unashamedly, phallic. Born from an epoch in which the survival of clan and tribe was dependent upon fertility, this may even define the power of a god. In our time, toxic masculinity has become a form of psychological plague and it can seem difficult to absorb such attributes of a god. We no longer have to hunt for our day-to-day survival, and going to war for the tribe (or nation state) is now not merely regressive but a threat to the continued survival of all life.

Our gods, recovered from beneath layers of time and civilisation, may bring with them a potency that we need, but that needs to be balanced with feminine energies, or else it can run out of control and become poisonously excessive. At the same time, men in particular need the gods to return. In some ways we have become too civilised, too bound by bricks and technology and the demands of our jobs to recall what we are as men, to recover, learn and live out what masculinity could genuinely mean. To become benevolent warriors, perhaps, protectors of our communities and fighters for justice. With the wildness of gods in our hearts.

Philip Kane is an author and poet, storyteller and artist; he is also the lineage holder for a Craft tradition rooted in the south east of England.

Nature Gods

Ellen Evert Hopman

I have been blessed to meet the Horned God in person a number of times. Many people seem to associate Him with rampant sexual energy but I have rarely experienced Him as the randy little Goat-footed God of the Greeks, nor has he seemed especially "horny" to me in a sexual sense. He has mostly shown Himself to me in his dignified, cosmic persona. In a recent encounter Cernunnos, a Western European Horned God, appeared right in front of me, staring directly into my eyes. He had ruddy skin, long, dark brown hair, and beautiful stag's antlers sprouting from His head. He seemed to feel great affection for me and as I looked at Him, I said: "Oh, you have brown eyes, just like me!" and He smiled.

One of the oldest images we have of the Horned God comes from the Indus Valley (in what is now Pakistan) in about the third millennium BCE, from the Harappan culture. He is depicted seated on the earth or on a small stool with His legs in "yogic" posture, both heels touching. He is nude and festooned with necklaces and bracelets. There are plant-like growths between His horns and He is accompanied by beasts; elephant, buffalo, tiger and rhinoceros. Two deer pose at His feet. The Harappan culture also left us images of Horned Goddesses, one of whom is shown in a tree, being worshipped by women and by a man with the body of a goat.

The Harappan Lord of the Animals evolved into the later Vedic "Shiva" who is called *"Prasupati"* (Lord of Beasts) and worshipped as a fertility God as well as a creator and destroyer of worlds. Shiva is also known as *"Ardhanarishwara"* (a half-male and half-female, hermaphrodite), Shiva/Shakti, and the Divine Androgyne. In His role as the Cosmic Dancer, he wears a serpent around His neck and is often shown in union with His female consort, Parvati, or Mother Nature.

Hinduism, which grew out of Vedic culture, sometimes describes Ultimate Reality as the union of *Shiva* (Divine Masculine Energy) and *Shakti* (Divine Female Energy). It is said that Shiva, the *Mahadeva* (Great God) and Pure Consciousness, has power only because of His devotion to Shakti. Shiva/ Shakti is in essence the force that breaks down matter so that new energies and objects can come into existence, and also continually re-creates all things anew.

This melding of the divine male energy and female energy has relevance when we examine the Horned God as He appears on the later European *Gundestrup* Cauldron, a metal cauldron of Celtic provenance that was found in a Danish peat bog. The most fascinating aspect of the Cernunnos depicted on it is the strong resemblance to the *Prasupati* seals from Harappan culture discussed above. On the Cauldron S/he is shown with stag horns, wearing a neck-ring (called a torc) that indicates noble status. S/he holds another torc in one hand and grasps a ram-headed serpent in the other. Of interest is the fact that this figure seems androgynous (other figures on the cauldron are either obviously female or wear beards). S/he is clean shaven and sitting in the half lotus yogic pose. S/he is surrounded by many types of animals including a lion, a dog or wolf, and a dolphin. One theory is that the Cauldron was made by itinerant metal workers from the East. Could this be a European variant of Shiva/Shakti?

Images of the Horned God survive from many European places and cultures. The church took special pains to erase His worship; even going so far as to turn him into "the Devil" (the Biblical Lucifer is a shining bright angel who has nothing to do with horns). Images of horned Goddesses are rarer, possibly due to the deliberate destruction of these and other Goddess images by the church.

The Horned God has been found on prehistoric Danish rock carvings. A bronze pin from Gotland, circa eighth century BCE features a snake topped by a human head with bull horns, the classic horns and snake conjunction that we also have from the Gundestrup Cauldron and early Harrapan images and images of Shiva as discussed above.

By the fourth century BCE we begin to find horned Gods in a Celtic context. In Northern Italy at *Val Camonica* there is a rock carving that shows a huge antlered figure next to a smaller (human?) figure with a tail. Horned figures have also been found in German areas and ancient antlered deities occur in Spain. The Horned God has been found in greatest concentration near Hadrian's Wall, in Scotland. He is also depicted all over Great Britain, Ireland, and Gaul (present day France). Sometimes He is shown as a "Janiform" figure, with two faces; once facing backwards and one facing forward, possibly relating to His ability to work in This world and in the Spirit world simultaneously, and to his dominion over the forces of change and transformation.

Cernunnos is one of the most popular horned deities for modern Pagans on a Celtic path. His name was inferred from an inscription found on a relief in Paris that reads *"--ernunnos"*. In the first century CE Gaulish sailors erected a monument to Him, possibly in the year 14 when Tiberius became emperor. The dedication was discovered in 1710 under the Cathedral of Notre Dame, the site of the capitol of the Celtic *Parisii* tribe. The monument depicts Cernunnos with Roman Gods such as Jupiter, Vulcan, Castor and Pollux. Two other plaques were found in the territory of the Celtic *Treveri* tribe in Luxembourg. Both are inscribed; *"Deo Ceruninco"* (to the God *Cerunincos*). Another Gaulish inscription found in Monatgnac reads; *"Carnonos"*.

The root word *"ker"* (head or protrusion) is found in every Indo-European dialect, from India to Ireland. Old Celtic *"Karnu"* means horn while *"on-os"* may mean lord or "great-man".

"*Cornu*" is Latin for horn, giving us the word "cornucopia". "*Kérnenos*" is Greek for "horned". Cernunnos is sometimes shown with a cornucopia, a symbol of plenty.

In Romano-Gaulish iconography Cernunnos sometimes appears flanked by Mercury and Apollo. He has a bag of grain or coins in His lap that spills before Him. A stag and bull at His feet eat the spilled grain indicating that He is Lord of both wild and domestic animals, linked to prosperity, and strong herds which are wealth on the hoof (as it were). Gaulish statues sometimes show him feeding ram-horned serpents. Serpents, like dragons, are guardians of treasure. The serpents that are shown with Cernunnos sometimes have fish tails. (There is a wonderful example in the Meigle museum in Perthshire, Scotland) Perhaps Cernunnos is also Lord of the treasures of the Sea.

Gaulish statues sometimes feature holes in the head of the Cernunnos figure, meaning that the figure had detachable horns. Horned animals like deer shed their antlers and re-grow them yearly, making Cernunnos a God of summer and winter, of shift and change. Coupled with the Janus headed aspect he is a God of powerful dualities; tame and wild beasts, the procession of the seasons, domestic herds and hunted animals, death and life, as well as protection for all of these and of prosperity for everyone; farmers, sailors, and those who call on Him. If we add in the vegetation imagery that sometimes accompanies His depiction, He is also Lord of the vegetation that sprouts in spring, grows tall in summer and is shed, like an antler, or cut like the grain, in fall and winter.

Horned Goddess images have also been found. These usually feature antlers rather than other types of horns. A Gaulish bronze antlered Goddess from Clermont-Ferrand sits cross legged holding a cornucopia. A horned Goddess image was found on local pottery from Richborough, Kent, dating to the first century CE. There is a stone carving of a Goddess from

Ribchester, Lancashire, which has horns. In Irish myths it was said that the *Mórrigan* could shape shift into stag form. The Irish Goddess *Flidais* was called "Mistress of Stags" and traveled in a chariot drawn by deer. *Elen* was the Green Woman; an antlered Goddess from Britain who appeared dressed in green leaves with a dog at Her side. Sometimes the Horned God is shown with a consort. One example is at *Aquae Sulis* (Bath) in England where a divine couple are depicted; a horned God and consort with three hooded figures and a ram.

There are a number of other horned Gods from Celtic tradition. The Celtic God *In Daghda*, who is skilled in every Druidic art, is sometimes shown with horns and in England we have Herne the Hunter who is associated with the death of stags in winter. He leads the Wild Hunt, a phantom horse race that occurs during stormy weather in winter and especially during the twelve days of Yule. He is the Spirit who guards Windsor Forest and appears in times of national crisis to guide and inspire the sacred warriors. Sylvanus is an antlered God of the forest associated with the hunt and with wild places. As Divine Hunter he is often depicted naked.

Cocidius (The Red One) is a British hunting God who is also a warrior God. A sacred tribal protector deity, he is a "ram-headed" God rather than an antlered one. *Camulos* was another ram-headed God who gave His name to the town of *Camulodunum* (modern Colchester). *Belatucadros* (Fair Shining One, Fair Slayer) was a ram-headed Warrior God from North Britain who was worshipped by foot soldiers, the Romans equated Him with Mars. Celtic warriors often wore horned helmets to emulate and honor these deities.

Depictions of the Horned God have been found near Hadrian's Wall in Scotland that show Him naked or wearing only a cloak, with His foot on a stone. In these depictions He sports goat horns. In ancient Wales great warriors were once called "bull-protectors" and "Bull Chieftains" while in Gaul a bull-horned God was shown with a purse, serpents, and a ram, apparently a protector of the flocks and of the wealth of the tribes.

The first time I met the Horned God He took me by surprise because as a follower of the Celtic and Druidic path the last deity I expected to *see* was Pan. He showed himself to me in a full-blown vision while meditating. I *saw* a dark night in the forest with a full moon directly overhead. There was a lake in the midst of a thick circle of trees, which must have been evergreens as they appeared impenetrable. Suddenly and slowly all the Gods and Goddesses started to appear, holding hands and dancing barefoot in a circle around the lake. They were colorfully attired in togas and cloaks of many hues.

There was one very tall figure, far taller than the rest, whose back was always towards me. He was holding hands in the circle with the other Gods but He was dancing a complicated reel that resembled an Irish step dance. He was dark skinned with huge horns that looked like antelope horns and very muscular. I received the inner message that He was the Great God Pan and that it was His dance that actually kept the universe moving. Without His dance the water would freeze and the leaves would never grow or turn colors in the fall. His dance was what kept the air moving and the planets and the solar systems and constellations in motion. He was Life and he was all movement; growth, change, and transformation.

Another encounter happened very recently. I had just come from a Sufi gathering where we had sung and danced and prayed to Allah. As I was driving away from the very warm and loving group of worshippers a stag appeared right next to my car, parallel to it, so close that I could see its eyes. I thought to myself "OK, Cernunnos, I haven't forgotten you, even IF I just went Sufi dancing". Next thing I knew a second stag appeared again, right next to my car. I gave thanks for the beauty and majesty of the vision and pondered on the great mystery that *all* the Gods are alive and with us all the time.

The Irish word for blessing is *"beannacht"* and the word for horn or antler is *"beann"*. When you bless someone in Gaelic you literally are saying "horns to/at you". May the Horned Gods and Goddesses bless us and everything in the great circle of creation forever!

Ellen Evert Hopman is the author of a number of books and has been a teacher of Herbalism since 1983 and of Druidism since 1990. She is currently Archdruid of Tribe of the Oak an international Druid teaching Order based in New England, USA.

Shamanic Gods

Kenn Day

My relationship with the gods was framed by my parent's choices. I was raised in a fundamentalist sect that prophesied the "end times," which were supposed to hit us around 1975. This gave me a sense of the divine masculine as a weirdly inconsistent and abusive parent, one who knew my innermost thoughts and condemned me for them. It was not a perspective that lent itself to any sort of mystical endeavor. You either toed the line and subjugated yourself to this omniscient and invisible god, or you grew up, and realized that these were the ravings of a narcissistic cult leader, and probably had nothing at all to do with God, if there even was such a thing.

It wasn't until I was well into my teens that I began to move past the restrictions of my upbringing and encounter other forms of spirituality. I began dabbling in ceremonial magic, which introduced me to the idea that there was a multiplicity of gods who could be summoned, appealed to, and negotiated with on any number of subjects. Because of my early experience of god as a bombastic, unforgiving bully, I was less than sanguine about the concept of invocation, and yet it did call to me. I didn't manage to find reputable teachers when I began. I made some unwise decisions, but I survived them.

The Neo-Pagan Festival movement was just accelerating when I discovered it, and I found myself invoking the god Pan around pagan bonfires to the throbbing accompaniment of live drums and whirling naked dancers. I could tell that the invocation had worked, because, although I felt wildly intoxicated, I could drink a whole bottle of rough red wine with no ill effect. And my whole demeanor was transformed.

Fortunately, though I hadn't managed to find a decent

teacher for these things in the ordinary world, I was blessed with what we call in Shamanism a spirit ally. The sense of the divine I received from Grandfather was that of a sometimes-motley crew of elder colleagues, who may or may not have my best interests at heart. I learned that it is always better to get to know the individual, no matter how divine, before making any commitments. From this Shamanic perspective, gods come in several flavors. There is God, a sort of universal awareness that abides as the underlying nature of all that is, but She doesn't really show up as an entity with whom we can converse. Since shamans tend to be focused on those spirits they can communicate, negotiate, and develop relationships with, we tend to be more interested in those who are considerably removed from her.

Those spirits who dwell in the realm of the gods tend to fall into certain categories. There are the ones that arise from distant, venerated ancestors, who have become larger with each generation. There are those mythical figures who have arisen from those archetypal forces' we humans have personified in the form of gods. These are ones like Poseidon, Hades, Thor, etc. There are the ones who begin as the spirits of a particular place or tribe and who then gain prominence as the human culture that birthed them becomes more dominant. Finally, there are those spirits who come to our world from elsewhere and set up house here as superior beings. The most apparent case of these are the Anunnaki, who became the gods of Sumer and later of Akkad, Babylon, and Chaldea. It is this last grouping that my patron Enki Comes from.

Grandfather's approach to building a relationship with a god was considerably more responsible and cautious than what I had done with Pan. He suggested that I research Enki -- get to know him -- before introducing myself directly. This was all pre-Google, so it meant many trips to the library. What I discovered when I started digging was a lot of spurious information about the Anunnaki as space aliens from a mysterious planet. This was based on supposed translations of ancient clay tablets that were debunked. But it did point to the nature of the Anunnaki as "not of this world".

From more scholarly sources I learned that Enki is the Sumerian god of water, knowledge (gestú), mischief, crafts (gašam), and creation (nudimmud), and one of the Anunnaki. He was later known as Ea in Akkadian and Babylonian mythology.

The next step on Grandfather's protocol was to begin developing a relationship with the entity by making regular offerings and asking for his attention. I made an altar to Enki and began burning incense and leaving gifts of milk and honey for him as part of my daily practice. After some months I began to have a sense that I was actually connecting with "something" as I made the offerings. This in itself was a bit unsettling, since I still wasn't sure that Grandfather was real, much less anything resembling a "god". Grandfather then suggested that I Journey to the Upper World to meet Enki directly. It took me awhile to understand what he was asking me to do, and even longer to agree to it. I had made countless Journeys to the Upper World by then, so that wasn't the issue. It was just the idea of meeting a "god" that had me stymied.

Eventually I made the usual deal with my ego, along the lines of "I don't have to acknowledge the reality of what I am about to experience," and I headed up the tree. Grandfather led me to an ornate door set into a high wall, where he told me to enter and explore -- with great respect. I opened the door and walked into a lovely garden, with a winding path that led me to a small gazebo. The structure sheltered what I took to be a statue of a winged figure. I realized that this was Enki and sat down to wait. I waited for quite some time and then came back a few more times before anything happened. On perhaps my fourth visit, the stature began to glow until it became so bright that I could no longer look at it. I could also feel a powerful presence rapidly approaching. As the glow dimmed, I was able to make out Enki as a tall distinguished figure, but I still couldn't ascertain any details. That first time, all I did was receive his presence. It didn't occur to me to make conversation. Over the next few visits, I began to ask questions and get to know him. I visited Enki several more times before opening a door to him on his altar and inviting him to enter my space. His presence was much less intense this way, but I could still feel him.

A couple years later, I was asked to invoke a god for a ritual at Spiral gathering, and chose to call in Enki. I had already learned to invoke, as noted earlier, but I worked with Grandfather to develop a stronger practice, calling in Enki regularly for a month before the event. I would invite him into my sacred space and then open myself to his embrace, allowing him to superimpose his presence on mine and then observe from the passenger seat before asking him to let me drive again. Grandfather stipulated that I was NOT to allow Enki or anyone else to take over entirely, because I was still responsible for the actions of my body, even if I wasn't in control. Also, I was to treat him with respect and only invite him in and then ask him to leave. There was to be none of the medieval summoning and banishing that I had learned in ceremonial work.

During this time, I composed an invocation to Enki to recite during the ritual. I focused on what I knew of him, both from research and from our interactions, and on the traits I wanted him to express when he arrived. Then I practiced inviting him in. At first it was more subtle than what I had experienced with Pan and some other deities, but the presence gradually become more substantial, as if it was waking up within me. By the time the festival was due to begin, I felt quite prepared.

I don't have a clear memory of the beginning of the ritual, only that we were gathered around the bonfire and I was dressed in a sarong and adorned with spirals of body paint. I carried a large shallow copper bowl filled with milk and honey, an offering to Enki. I paced slowly around the fire as I recited the invocation, feeling him draw nearer and nearer. The sky was already overcast when we began, but when I completed the invocation, lifting the offering bowl above my head, the sky opened and it began to rain heavily. The sensation of the cold rain against my skin "awakened" Enki within me and he proceeded to whirl ecstatically and bestow blessings on all those who still braved the elements.

The aftermath of the ritual and the release of Enki is vague in my memory. There is usually a sense of gradually awakening from something akin to a dream state, with less memory of the experience than you might expect. The exhilaration gives way to a heaviness and exhaustion. It is always a good idea to bring yourself fully back into your physical body and ordinary state of consciousness by eating and otherwise engaging your five senses.

Enki has remained my primary divine patron over the past few decades, and my practice of invoking him has evolved. But the fundamentals remain the same and apply to any spirit -- divine or otherwise -- that you would consider inviting in. Don't expect to play with the gods without consequences. Treat them with respect. Introduce yourself and get to know them before attempting to deepen the relationship. In much the same way that there are people who you wouldn't want to have in your house, be aware that there are spirits you don't want to develop a relationship with, much less invite to share your body. When it is time to separate from the spirit, thank them and then you withdraw. You are not "banishing" them, but moving yourself away and apart from them.

The impact of invoking a god depends on the nature of the entity invoked. Whatever that nature is, you can generally learn from it, receive blessings and empowerment from it, and it will leave an impression that can and will transform you.

Invocation to Enki

Ride to me on the wings of storm
From earth and sky at once to me
I am your vessel and your voice
Lord of the earth
And laughing god
I echo your name through song and verse
I spill myself upon your earth
I fill myself from your embrace
You are the water and the wine
Of running cloud and scarlet meal
Of blood and soil beneath the earth
Still roaming deep forgotten rooms
To skry the moon – to tell the tale
Of your daughter's courage and her fear
To pass alone these gates
That hold the invocation of return

Here lies my name
In nameless stance
Upon this twilight floor entranced
By passages beyond these lands of men
And dreams of careless gods

Enki, Ea, Enochi
I call you by the writhing names
Of the water and the earth
I summon you to dance with me
Again to turn this wheel
Of life – of blood – of wine and spin
The answers from my mind
To trust – to laugh – to fill my soul
With your wisdom and your dream
That this magic will not die

That slumbers here within my heart
But rise instead to the Dru's recall
To remember me in all my age
By all my names
For I am Enki once again

Enki, Enki, Enkidu
Who spent himself
Beneath the fall of Gilgamesh
And plundered Tiamat's darkened womb
Who pulled Innana from the grasp
Off Ereshkigal in her bitter tomb
And washed her feet in the tears
Of goddesses and gods

Would you forget
The taste of me upon the rain
The solid tramp of earthen feet
This is my call
This is my song
Awaken to me
Who would hear this spell
That I may dwell again
Within this world of magic
And of men.

For I am Enki, Enki! IAO Ea!
Enki ehya! Enochi!

Kenn Day is a working shaman, with a full-time practice since 1989. He is the author of *Dance of Stones* and *Post-Tribal Shamanism*.

Mad About the Boy

Robin Herne

Late in October in the year 130CE a young man around the age
of 19 or 20 fell headlong into the River Nile where he drowned.
It remains a mystery to all but time travellers and those in the
direct confidence of Antinous himself whether he leapt willingly
to his death as either a suicide or self-sacrificial offering, or
plunged by accident, or was shoved by a murderous hand.
Despite his tender years, Antinous had made political enemies
by winning the devoted love of the Emperor Hadrian.

The upper class Athenian model of sexual relationships was
of an older, wiser, richer, cultured *erastes* initiating a younger,
unsophisticated *eromenos* into the ways of the world. Romans,
such as Hadrian, were much influenced by Athenian culture
– when he first met Antinous the lad was a teenager and the
emperor a middle-aged man (a relationship that would be
illegal in most parts of the world today, and which looms as a
moral cloud in terms of the relationship between ancient and
modern pagan values). The children of the wealthy were, to a
large extent, sheltered from the adult world outside the home
and so this relationship became a way of educating people
about how to behave in polite society. Athenians held a 10-year
age gap as ideal, though there are many accounts of bigger age
differences (such as between Antinous and Hadrian). Wealthy
men were not expected to marry till later in life, and to marry
a younger woman when they finally did so. The woman was
expected to be sheltered, naïve, unworldly etc. and it was the
duty of the husband to simultaneously shelter her but also teach
her to become the doughty matriarch who would one day run
his household and exert the sort of influence that was satirised
by Aristophanes in *Lysistrata*. It seems fairly evident that the

famed poetess Sappho had much the same relationships with younger women. Those men like Hadrian had the same kind of relationship with his own sex.

The primary difference between a same-sex and a different-sex relationship in Athens, Sparta and other parts of the Classical world was duration. Heterosexual marriage was assumed to be for life, whilst two men (or two women) in the *erastes-eromenos* relationship were expected to become "just good friends" when the younger partner reached the point of establishing their own career or household. Antinous died before reaching marriageable age, and Hadrian was distraught. Egyptian tradition identified those who died in the Nile with Asur (whom the Greeks called Osiris), which may have led many people along the banks of the great river to reverence the dead youth. Perhaps word reached the mourning emperor, for he soon came to believe that Antinous had become translated into the realm of the Olympus. Temples were built in honour of the new god all over the empire, a constellation was named after him (which was only renamed Aquila the Eagle in 1930, for reasons one can but speculate upon), even an entire city built and named after him – Antinopolis – in Egypt, now reduced to rubble. A comparable deity who was also translated into a constellation was Ganymede (who is also patronym to a moon of Jupiter), cup-bearer of Zeus, who was immortalised as Aquarius. He too was regarded as a mortal son of Troy, with various regal parents attributed by different authors.

Hadrian instigated an annual celebration for his deceased lover, the Antinoeia, in late October – presumably on the anniversary of the drowning. A large gathering, it was celebrated with various sporting and artistic competitions. As time rolled on the festivals also developed an allegedly orgiastic side, to the disgust of church dignitaries and some pagan philosophers alike (the latter often echoing the views of Epicurus that it was better to keep dignified moderation and self-control with one's pleasures than to give in to wild abandon). Whilst the distant past was not quite the sexual free-for-all that some people fantasise about, many cultures were far more willing to allow people to find the love or pleasure without the level of disapproval and often murderous policing that has taken place under monotheism. The distaste of some philosophers with what they considered excessive self-indulgence should not be confused with oppression or brutality. There are groups of modern polytheists and pagans who continue to mark the Antinoeia in various different ways.

A number of interesting points arise from this situation. That Antinous was a real, historical person is not in dispute. A number of religions have central figures who were mortals raised to divine or semi-divine status. Given that some of these religions have a contentious relationship with paganism, it is not overly surprising that a number of modern pagans are wary about the notion of a deified human. Even the ancient world was a trifle surprised at the reverencing of Antinous, although this was for reasons of social class – the translation of mortal to god was almost entirely reserved for royalty. That a commoner should receive this status may well have seemed shocking.

17th century China gives us the story of a young soldier, Hu Tianbao, who fell in unrequited love with an imperial dignitary whose name is not recorded. Social class divides once again reared their head and, when the dignitary not only heard that he was being mooned over by a low-status soldier but actually caught the man peeking at him in the bathhouse, he ordered his flunkies to beat Hu Tianbao to death. The disconsolate soul arrived before the Judge of the Dead, the Taoist deity Yama who heard the tale of his death as was customary. Yama declared that anyone who died for love did not deserve to be in the hellish realms, but should be sent up to put his case before the August Jade Emperor. The head of the celestial realms decided to transform the soldier into a divinity, granting him the new name of Tu Er Shen, the Little Rabbit God. The writer Yuan Mei recorded that villagers in the Fujian Province (where the soldier had lived and died) began to dream about the Rabbit God. The deification here is in the hands of the existing deities, but backed up by popular acclaim fuelled by visionary experiences. The issue of deification is one that needs re-evaluation in modern polytheism. Neither of these two men, nor the other cases to shortly be mentioned, were particularly holy or saintly people – their translation to the spirit realm did not occur because of an outstanding degree of inner goodness. It is perhaps the influence of Christianity that encourages the assumption that those declared sacred should be people of overt goodness and compassion.

By what process does a mortal become divine? The process of canonisation in the Catholic Church is clear and well-documented, but in the ancient world it is very unclear. That Hadrian wanted the cult started was undoubtedly a central driving force, but the local Egyptian populace most likely started the adoration of Antinous by popular grassroots acclaim, inspired chiefly by the cause of death.

In neither the Taoist nor the Romano-Greek cases is a hierarchical priesthood seen to regulate who or what can become a figure of reverence. Understanding the process of apotheosis is not merely an academic issue, but one of relevance to the modern community. The 17th century is not so far away, and if new deities could arise as recently as that what is to say that pagans alive today may not one day have temples to dedicated to them, prayers and petitions addressed to them? Much is made of paganism being a nature religion with deities of mountain, river, and forest. The ancients recognised that humans too were part of the natural order and as much potential figures of spiritual devotion as an oak tree or a wolf. Sociologists might well suggest that we have processes of what might be turned secular deification in which movie stars, royalty, pop stars and others are elevated to figures of post-mortem devotion ad adulation. It may well be that, to paraphrase Carl Jung, we have a demigod-shaped hole in the human collective consciousness that craves ancestral figures be they ancient warriors, imperial boyfriends, or Hollywood starlets.

Of less certain historicity is the figure of Hyacinthus, a warrior of Sparta who so inspired Apollo that the radiant god began what was purportedly the very first male romance with him. As befits the Greek style of relationship, Apollo schooled the mortal youth in many military skills and other arts. The intensity of their love was such that it drove the wind spirit Zephyrus mad with jealousy. Unable to bear his invidia any longer, the west wind blew a heavy discus off-course which fractured the skull of Hyacinthus. Unable to heal the fatal wound, Apollo took his soul to Olympus and caused a plant to grow from the pool of blood. The plant is usually given as the hyacinth, but some linguists have argued that the original word actually meant a larkspur. There is no direct mention of local community members having dreams of Hyacthinus after his death, but this does not mean that popular acclaim may not have had a strong role to play in the move to enshrine him. In essence Hyacinthus becomes a god because he is beloved by one, which raises the frequent theme in Classical mythology of deities taking a sexual interest in humanity. Most demigods come into existence when a male deity impregnates a mortal woman. Polytheist religions are obviously not the only ones to have such a relationship as a prominent part of their mythology, though they appear to be the only one to have same sex deity-mortal romances within their repertoire of tales.

The Spartans devoted a three-day festival in June to honour their hero, the Hyacinthia. The first day was one of ritualistic mourning for the death, the second a joyful celebration of rebirth, and the third purportedly a day for mysteries. The festivities were shared with Apollo whose statue was dressed with a freshly woven garment. Whilst pre-Raphaelite art tends to portray Hyacinthus as a simpering pretty boy, it must be remembered that Spartan warriors were as tough as nails from childhood onwards and preferred snarling to simpering! Whilst some Spartans may have petitioned for aid with romantic matters, they were just as likely to call to Hyacinthus for victory in battle. The modern perception of gay men as feminine, camp, or simply very gentle would mean little to this spiritual entity. He challenges modern assumptions and political stereotypes.

Controversial art historian Camille Paglia is one of many to have commented on the persistent and widespread cult of the beautiful youth, which remained in art long after it had been suppressed in religion. The worship of youth and beauty tends to be widespread, regardless of whether female or male, whilst the charms of maturity and wisdom seldom have quite such popular appeal. She suggests that a great deal of Western artistic culture (and maybe she would have suggested Eastern too, had she been considering figures such as Tu Er Shen) has been driven by gay men. She argues that many such men have served a cerebral function in society, freed from family commitments with wives and children, they have invested their energies in music, art, science, literature and so forth. Perhaps a little idealised at times, it is nonetheless an argument that might have theological application – that these deities are less concerned with lustiness than they are with innovation, aesthetic beauty, and creativity.

The worship of some of these gods has revived in modern times. At least one temple to Tu Er Shen now exists in Taiwan, where its founder and priest Lu Wei-ming conducts same-sex wedding blessings. Increasing numbers of gay and bisexual men of East Asian descent are rediscovering the fact that they too once had a place amongst the gods and someone to stand guardian over them. Filmmaker Andrew Huang produced a beautiful short movie about him in 2019, in which the deity manifests to a repressed Chinese restaurant worker in modern America. Antinous also has a number of shrines around the world, both physical ones and virtual online ones, and even makes a brief appearance in Neil Gaiman's novel, American Gods.

In a newspaper interview Lu Wei-ming described how many thousands of gay people visit the shrine each year to seek the rabbit god's aid with their love lives. This is a positive sign of how important this god is to many, but also raises the concern that deities such as Antinous, Hyacinthus, and Tu Er Shen have been labelled as "gay gods" effective meaning that they are only of interest to homosexual and bisexual men. Baldr and Perun are not labelled as "straight gods" only of interest to heterosexuals; their devotion is not confined to boxes by needless fences. The way we label deities is reflective of the way we identify ourselves and risk ghettoising religious practices. Historically, deities such as Antinous and Tu Er Shen are open to devotion from anyone regardless of sexuality or gender. Whether modern day heterosexual people see any great purpose in devoting themselves to deities such as these remains to be seen, but it is worth bearing in mind that such entities do not confine themselves to solitary issues such as helping people with their love lives.

Much mythology presents most deities as timeless, ancient beings emerging with the mountains, oceans, and forests. With Hyacinthus, Tu Er Shen, Antinous and various others we find deities decidedly late to the stage. The polytheologist, if such a clumsy portmanteau can be used, might account these as simply the latest incarnations of much older presences. Equally, they might conceive of the human soul as a divine spark – the genius of Roman pneumatology – which might, given the correct circumstances, flower into a demigod after death. Late blooming deities open up the possibility of overseeing guardians for new technologies and ways of being.

What then are Antinous and Tu Er Shen – are they actual deities on a par with Cernunnos or Thor, or are they archetypes of the Eternal Youth, or historical persons whose names have been deployed to serve a socio-political agenda after their deaths? Perhaps they are a combination of all of the above. If there is even a spark of divinity at the core of these devotional figures, then they present a challenge to a world which is still, even in the 21st century, more inclined to condemn love between two men as devilish rather than divine.

Contemporary forms of paganism often make extensive use of myths involving heterosexual couples as a basis for ritual drama – the devotion of God to Goddess. There are other permutations which could also be considered as celebratory templates for understanding the world and our place within it. The death-and-apotheosis sagas of the Hyacinthia, the Antinoeia, or of Tu Er Shen could engage worshippers as readily as better known stories.

Robin Herne is an educator, poet, storyteller, poet, artist, dog-owner and Druid. He has written numerous articles for Pagan magazines, has appeared in television documentaries and is the author of a number of books including *Old Gods, New Druids*, and *Pantheon – The Egyptians*.

Gods of London

Lucya Starza

London still honours its old, Pagan gods. Underneath twenty-first century offices lies the temple of an ancient mystery cult. Leaving the busy, city streets, you walk through its doors and down steps, through layers of earth revealing the secret signs of centuries past, and enter the ancient Temple of Mithras. The sights and sounds of worship greet you.

Torches on pillars dimly light the chamber, which is lined by benches for you and your brothers in the cult to sit. You can hear them chanting, as the mysteries are enacted at the altar at the far end. This is only a reconstruction of Mithraic worship in historic times, shown through sound, and light, and haze. Back in Roman times, as a woman, I would not have been allowed into this exclusively male space of worship, honouring a god depicted slaughtering a bull and banqueting, with images of the sun, the moon and the zodiac in scenes carved on the walls.

The Temple of Mithras was rediscovered in 1954, but it was originally built on the bank of the river Walbrook in the mid-third century, when London – or Londinium – was a Roman city. Mithras, a god associated with the sun, justice, contracts and warfare, was originally a Persian deity, but his cult was spread across the empire by Roman soldiers, to whom his mysteries appealed.

Archaeologists found that the London Mithraeum was later rededicated to Bacchus, the god of wine, in the early fourth century, who was worshipped by both men and women. Lead weights depicting maenads – frenzied female followers of the god of wine and ecstasy – have been found nearby, along with other depictions of Bacchus. Statues of other deities have also found at the Walbrook site, including a head of Serapis,

Egyptian god of the underworld; a statue of the Mercury, god of commerce, the head and shoulders of a river god – perhaps representing Neptune or the Thames, and other statuettes of deities, both Roman and Romano-Celtic. One that is currently in the Museum of London, along with many of the statues from the Temple of Mithras, might even represent the spirit of London itself. The Walbrook was, without doubt, a religious centre for those who visited, lived and traded in Londinium.

The Roman Temple of Mithras reopened in 2017 by communication corporation Bloomberg. Although it is not a place where modern Pagans can worship, it offers a hint of what it was like when Romans did, through a sound and light performance that repeats at regular intervals throughout the day. The temple is seven metres below the streets of modern London. A mezzanine, directly above, introduces it with interactive displays that invite visitors to explore the practices and symbols associated with the cult of Mithras. At street level is an exhibition of more than 600 Roman artefacts found during excavations as Bloomberg's offices were built. You can visit the London Mithraeum, at 12 Walbrook, London EC4N, free of charge from Tuesday to Sunday until 6pm, although advance booking is recommended.

Raven Gods of London

But London has gods older than Mithras or his fellow Roman imports. Long before the city existed, our ancestors venerated ancient gods on the banks of the Thames and the surrounding marshland. The oldest effigy was discovered in Rainham Marshes. It is one of earliest carved figures found in Britain, dating from about 2250 BCE, and is known as the Dagenham Idol. Cut from the wood of the evergreen Scots pine, with what appears to be one blind eye, this could possibly be an early representation of the god Odin, Norse god of wisdom, divination and magic, who sacrificed his eye in his quest for knowledge. Archaeologist Bryony Coles has pointed out that the Dagenham Idol is similar to others found in wetlands in Britain, Ireland and Scandinavia. Odin, like the Dagenham Idol, also has gender ambivalence. Although he is a god, some statues show him wearing female attire, and he was the master of a form of magic usually done by women. The Dagenham Idol has a hole between the legs, which might have been a peg for a long-lost penis, but might also mean this particular deity has the potential to be both male and female.

The statue, which was unearthed in 1922, is owned by Colchester Castle Museum, but is on indefinite loan to Valence House Museum, in Becontree Ave, Dagenham. You can also see a pair of replicas in the Museum of London, one of which is available to be handled.

Odin has two ravens: Huginn and Muninn, or thought and memory. However, he is not the only raven god of London. According to the Welsh myths of the Mabinogion, the head of king and guardian Bran the Blessed was buried on the white hill where the Tower of London now stands. Bran's head is said to magically protect the land. According to Boria Sax in *City of Ravens*, the name Bran 'means "crow" in Welsh, and "raven" in Cornish, Irish and Scots Gaelic'. Nowadays, the Tower of London is famously the home of ravens that are said to also offer magically protection against invasions. During the Second World War they did just that, being used as unofficial spotters for enemy bombs and planes. Boria Sax writes that the etymology of the word London could be a Roman version of the Celtic name 'Lugdunum', which possibly translates 'the town of ravens'. Another possible translation is 'the town of the god Lugh', which would connect the city to the Irish god of many talents. Peter Ackroyd, in *Thames: Sacred River* points to the mysterious god Ludd as being 'the Celtic divinity of the Londoners', and a potential name-connection with the city, although little is known about him. Iain Sinclair had earlier invoked the god in the title of his 1981 book *Lud Heat: A Book of the Dead Hamlets*, a mixture of poetry and prose about occult forces at work in the city.

God of the River

Old Father Thames is the god most associated with London, although the personification of the river that is the city's lifeblood is somewhat mysterious. The river is the reason people have inhabited the area since ancient times, the reason Romans founded Londinium in AD 43, and has helped London grow to be an internationally important city. The river and its tributaries have been worshipped since prehistory, as is shown by the offerings found in its waters and along its banks, including the Battersea Shield, which is now in the British Museum. It dates back to the Iron Age and is one of the most impressive examples of Celtic art found in England. Earlier than that, Neolithic people deposited polished flint maces in the river. Swords from the Bronze Age, Iron Age and Viking era have been found there. Even today, Hindus in London make offerings to the river they see as sacred.

Yet the Thames hasn't always been an old father. Roman sea trader Tiberinius Celerianus erected a plaque and possibly a statue to Mars Camulos – combining the Roman god of war with a Celtic deity thought to have been a guardian of the river. The head and shoulders of a statue found near the Temple of Mithras might represent the Thames, but might be Neptune, Roman god of fresh water and the seas.

But what about Old Father Thames? As Peter Ackroyd writes in his book on the river: 'Thames is an old name... It may spring from the primordial tribes of the Mesolithic or Neolithic periods who...shared a common language. The syllable *teme* may... indicate darkness, in the sense of holy or sacred fearfulness.' He suggests the Celts and Romans and Saxons might have kept its ancient name because it was numinous, but also writes that the figure and appearance of Old Father Thames has 'a striking resemblance to the tutelary gods of the Nile and Tiber.' There are many statues and sculptures of Old Father Thames in London, but none are ancient. One can be seen at St John's Lock, Lechlade, but was originally commissioned for the Crystal Palace in London, in 1854. There is one in Trinity Square, on the former headquarters of the Port of London Authority. Other representations can be seen at Somerset House, Ham House, Hammersmith Town Hall, Kew Bridge, Vauxhall Bridge and the riverbank at Nine Elms. They all date from recent centuries; the terracotta plaque at Nine Elms was put there in 1988. You will hear the name Old Father Thames invoked in pretty much any TV documentary about the river, and he is a contemporary god of London, even if his origin is lost in history.

Little Gods of London

From the mighty deity of the river, to the little gods of London: in the European room at the British Museum, and at the Museum of London, there are many tiny statuettes of deities honoured in Roman times. Among the many little figurines displayed are: Apollo, god of music, poetry, prophecy and light; Mercury, god of commerce; and Hermaphrodite, a mythological being who displays both male and female features. As the figurines are so small, they might have been used by individuals – perhaps carried around – to help them get through their busy days and deal with the problems they faced. Alternatively, they might have been left as offerings – some of the figures were found in the Thames.

Christianity came to Britain with the Romans, and was widespread after the fourth century. St Pancras Old Church claims to be on the site where Christ was first worshipped in an organised way in London, in the fourth century. Fragments of Roman material can even be spotted in the current building. Roman Londinium was largely abandoned in the fifth century, although there was a large Anglo-Saxon settlement nearby. Vikings raided the area and sometimes dwelt within the old walls. Many people living by the Thames returned to Paganism. When London once more became a city, Christianity was growing, with at least some churches built on the sites of former Pagan worship. Excavations at Southwark Cathedral, near London Bridge, unearthed a statue of a Romano-Celtic hunter god. His identity is unknown, but you can see a replica on display in the corridor outside the cathedral's excellent café.

In the eighteenth century, Pagan gods returned to London – and the rest of England – with artwork full of the gods and goddesses of ancient Rome becoming the latest fashion trend. One of the finest examples is the Painted Ceiling at the Old Royal Naval College in Greenwich, south east London, which depicts a mixture of allegorical, mythological, historical and contemporary characters. Deities, including Apollo, Bacchus, and Neptune, are used to symbolise natural forces and abstract concepts. Britain was a Protestant country, so the use of Pagan gods for this purpose was considered more appropriate than Catholic saints. Painted by Sir James Thornhill between 1707 and 1726, is intended to tell a story of political change and human achievements, rather than anything religious. But even if eighteenth century England wasn't a Pagan country, the fashion for classical mythology was influential in the start of the Pagan Revival. Even today, many atheist or agnostic Pagans regard deities as symbols and archetypes rather than living entities – not too different from the way some of our ancestors would have done in the 1700s.

The Ancient Egyptian sun god Ra found a home in London in the nineteenth century and became an important landmark. Better known as Cleopatra's Needle, the Obelisk of Ra was originally erected by Thutmoses III outside his temple of sun in the city of Heliopolis, Egypt, in 1450 BCE. It was moved to Alexandria under the orders of Cleopatra. In 1819, Egypt's then ruler, Muhammad Ali, gave the monument to the British government. It was brought to London in 1878 and erected on the banks of the Thames, where it still stands.

Another of London's most famous landmarks – the statue of a young, winged god with a bow and arrow, atop the fountain in Piccadilly Circus – also dates from the nineteenth century. These days most Londoners are aware that the statue isn't meant to represent Eros, the Greek god of desire. It was designed to be Anteros, god of selfless love, and was associated with charity rather than sex. It was created to commemorate the good works of nineteenth-century philanthropist the 7th Earl of Shaftesbury. Apparently English people struggled with the concept of there being many different types of love, so the statue's nickname of the more famous Eros stuck.

Io Pan!

Pan is a god with a varied reputation – and all his aspects can be found in London. In ancient Greece, Pan was a god of the wilderness and nature, but also of shepherds and pastures. He because associated with fertility and springtime – and with sex. His name is also the root of the word 'panic' and Pan was thought to also prompt sudden fear, making animals stampede and even causing mass panic in humans. Pan's gentler side can be seen in his namesake, Peter Pan, the 20th century fictional creation of writer JM Barrie. A statue of Peter Pan can be found in Hyde Park, where it was erected in 1912. However, horror writer Arthur Machen, in his story *The Great God Pan*, had a few years earlier envisaged the deity in his wilder, sexual form, bringing death and destruction to London society.

Pan was also important for the growth of modern Paganism. Egyptologist and University College, London, professor Margaret Murray, in her influential 1931 book *The God of the Witches*, theorised that Pan was a form of the horned god worshipped by a Pagan witch-cult surviving since ancient times. Although her theories are now largely discredited, her writings influenced the way Wiccans and other modern witches view the archetypal god of male virility connected to the cycles of the seasons.

Nowadays, there are many Pagan groups honouring the ancient gods of London. Some hold open rituals on the banks of the Thames, in the remnants of the ancient woods that surround the city, in their own homes or in public venues.

Lucya Starza is an eclectic witch living in London, England, with her husband and cats. She is the author of *Candle Magic, Poppets and Magical Dolls, Guided Visualisations* and *Scrying*. You can find her daily postings on A Bad Witch's Blog at www. badwitch.co.uk.

Part 2

Naming the God

INM (AMUN)

Jennifer Uzzell

Amun (meaning the 'hidden one') is first mentioned in The Pyramid texts of the 5th Dynasty as a member of the Ogdoad, a group of eight primordial deities arranged into four groups of male and female responsible for creation. He is usually represented as a man wearing a double-feathered crown, or as a ram, but has also been depicted as a goose, an ape or a man with the head of a frog or a crocodile. His origins are uncertain, possibly in Heliopolis, the centre of the Ogdoad, or in the Nubian centre of Gebel Barkel in North Sudan. Certainly, by the time of the 11th Dynasty, he had replaced Monthu, the falcon headed god of war as the patron god of Thebes. His consort was Amunet, a feminised form of the same name who may or may not ever have been seen as a separate deity.

The 11th Dynasty Pharaoh Ahmose I defeated the foreign Hyksos rulers during the 16th century BCE and re-established a unified Egypt with its capital at Thebes. As a result, Amun, as patron of Thebes, rapidly grew in status and importance and a programme of temple building in his honour was begun throughout the country, but especially at Luxor and Karnack. His consort became identified with Mut, whose name means 'mother' and who was associated with the primordial waters of creation. Together with their son, the moon god Khonsu, they were regarded as a holy family.

Amun means 'hidden' or secret' and he was regarded as a transcendent and unknowable god who has created the cosmos but remained apart from it. As he became more influential, however, he was syncretised with the sun god Re as Amun-Re. Re was the manifest and visible form of the divine and so Amun-Re represented the balance between God as unknowable and God as revealed and present. This appealed to Egyptian ideas of balance and may explain why Amun was associated with the concept of justice (Ma'at) and was seen as a defender of the poor and oppressed. One inscription to him contains the line, 'You are the Lord of the silent who comes at the voice of the poor.' Following the conquest of Nubia, he was identified with the chief god of Kush (Amarni) who was shown as a ram. The ram had obvious associations with fertility, leading to his further identification with the Egyptian fertility deity Min as Amun-Min. This form of Amun was celebrated at the Opet festival where his image was taken down the Nile from Karnack to Luxor to celebrate his marriage to Mut.

The priests of Amun became immensely powerful and at times, effectively rulers of Egypt whose power was as great, if not greater than that of the king. This led to conflict and was eventually influential in Akhenaten banning the worship of Amun and moving the capital, and his own cult of the Aten to Amarna. Following his death, however, worship of Amun was quickly restored and continued into the Hellenistic period.

ANGUS ÓG

Fiona Tinker

Most people will have heard of Angus Óg in the context of the Irish God of love, music and poetry; the younger son of The Dagda and the Goddess Boann, for whom the River Boyne is named. Irish myth states that Dagda desired Boann, so he sent her husband to a distant part of his kingdom whilst he seduced her. When Boann conceived, Dagda caused time to stand still; Angus was therefore conceived, gestated and born in one day. It is from this legend that his name arises: he is the 'Ever Young.' However, there is a less well-known side of Angus Óg; one that seems to be much older and to belong to a time when neither Scotland nor Ireland yet existed. Stories of Angus moved across those lands once known as the Kingdom of *Dal Riata*. The traditional role of the storytellers – the *seanchaidhean* – meant Angus's stories survived in various forms, not all of them fossilised in ink.

Who is he? Angus is a gentle God, a quiet, in the background sort of person, not one to push himself to the fore – unless necessary. His sword is called The Great Fury: that is no idle boast.

Irish tales say he is the fifth son of the Dagda and one who would not put himself forward for Kingship. He was happy as he was. Love, music and poetry are things he concerns himself with. But he has older concerns too. He is an Ever-Young God; but this is not the same as being young. He is not the pre-pubescent Eros depicted in some paintings. Angus has four white birds that fly around his head and these are his kisses. The rowan is sacred to him. He has the ability to transform, usually into a white swan, but some stories tell of other transformations. At various times, he has transformed as a white stag, white birds and a large purple and pink fly.

His other concerns are as a keeper of the keys to the Realms, making him a God of Life, Death and Rebirth; one interpretation of the three arms of the triple spiral with Angus himself holding the liminal space at the centre. He is well- known in Scotland as a seller of dreams and as a trickster. Many of the old Scottish tales expand on these traits, along with his other attributes.

He may be young, but he is no fool. He is an old God. Stories portray a deity who is hope eternal, the joy of life, a God of weather, seasons and growth. Brief comments on two old tales will serve as an introduction to this alternative guise.

The Awakening of Angus Óg: This rather nice little romantic tale gives some idea of the attributes and acknowledgement other Gods give to Angus. It also shows several patterns of three, which are important within Celtic mythology in general. Reading the metaphors in the story, Angus holds Lordship over the land, sea and sky. He has been here before they existed and he will be there long after they have gone. It is in the places where the edges of these three realms meet that Angus can be felt at his most powerful.

The Coming of Angus and Bride: This story picks up on Angus as God of Seasons, which is only hinted at in the first tale. Angus is actively engaged in battle with The Cailleach, the Old Woman of Winter and the Ancient Mother Goddess of Scotland. The symbolism is similar to that found in many other Pantheons; the Goddess of Spring must be rescued from the clutches of winter.

The movement of peoples between present-day Ireland and Scotland ensured tales of our ancient Gods and heroes reflected the landscapes and concerns of both countries. Gods transfer, grow and become absorbed into the culture of a new locality. The symbolism and metaphorical meanings in ancient tales are always worth thought and exploration, that is where the learning lives. Perhaps there has been a 'forgetting' of some of Angus's older aspects, but even as Angus slept for a thousand years as in the first tale, humanity did not forget him. How could we? His breath was in our kisses and his joy danced in our veins as we felt the year turn to the sun.

To honour Angus Óg, meditate in a place where the land, sea and sky meet. Or have these realms represented in your circle. You are respecting the arms of the triple spiral whose centre is Angus. He holds the keys to the realms.

He may come to you in the form of a bird, he may come to you in dreams, or he may come to you in feelings of sheer joy and life pulsing through you. You will know when you are Angus blessed.

ANUBIS – THE JACKAL GOD

David Rankine

Anubis (pronounced Anpu or Anup in Egyptian), is one of the oldest Egyptian gods, whose roots stretch far back past the pre-Dynastic age to the jackal shamans of c. 20,000 BCE, whose images were found in Egyptian caves in the twentieth century. Anubis was usually depicted as a jackal or wild dog-headed man, or a reclining black jackal. Anubis was the great protector god, guiding the soul through the underworld, and even protecting other gods during their disputes. He was also the Lord of embalming, and through this is connected with incense and perfumery.

Anubis is depicted as black-furred, the colour of night, and of death. Black symbolised the underworld, but could also symbolise resurrection, life and fertility (and in this respect was interchangeable symbolically with green).

Although his cult was recognised throughout Egypt, seen in the numerous chapels and depictions in mortuary temples and tombs, Anubis also possessed a localised focus as the chief god of the 17th Upper Egyptian nome in Middle Egypt, known to the Greeks as Cynopolis (*'the city of the dogs'*, modern el-Qeis).

The etymology of Anubis (*Anpw*) is uncertain, the most common attribution is a translation as *"royal child"*, which probably explains his title of *"King's son, greatest and first, Anubis"*. As is often the case with the ancient gods, the genealogy of Anubis is also unclear. The earliest references to parentage are to a mother only, either the cow goddess Hesat or the cat goddess Bastet. The Greek author Plutarch (45-120 CE) integrated Anubis into the Osirian mythos as the son of Osiris and Nephthys. The *Book of Caverns* (section four) refers to Anubis and Horus alike as sons of Osiris, and the *Jumilhac Papyrus* frequently characterizes Anubis as the son of Osiris and of Isis. Few, if any, of the familial relationships between Gods in Egyptian religion are fixed; instead, they follow from the functions accorded to a deity in a given time and context.

His titles tell us much about his nature and roles; these include:

- Hery Seshta (hry-sst3) – *"Master of Secrets"*, a title he subsequently shared with Thoth and Isis.
- Wer-Hekau (ur-hk3w) – *"Mighty One of Magic"*, another title shared with Thoth and Isis, again emphasising his role as a god of magic.
- As Tepy-dju-ef (tp.y ḏw=f) or *"He who is upon his mountain"* he watched from the desert cliffs overlooking the necropoles.
- Khenty-imentiu (ḫnty-jmnty.w) – *"Foremost of the Westerners"*: refers to the role of Anubis as leader of the "westerners"; that is, those that resided in the West, place of the dead.
- Neb ta-djeser (nb t3-ḏsr) – *"Lord of the Sacred Land/Lord of the Pure Land"* refers to the desert land around the necropoles.
- Imy-wut (jm.y-wt) – *"He Who is in the Place of Embalming"* – clearly refers to the central role of the Anubis in embalming.
- Heka-ped-wut (hq3-pd.wt) – *"Ruler of the Bows"*, referring to his control over negative forces, these being the Nine Bows which represented the symbolic enemies of Egypt.

Another major role of Anubis is that of key-holder, bearing the keys of the underworld. In the *Greek Magical Papyri*, he is referred to in this role a number of times, e.g., *"O thou Key-holder, guardian, Anubis. Send up to me the phantoms of the dead Forthwith for service in this very hour."*

In the Greco-Egyptian period, Anubis was particularly

associated with divination. One scrying spell calls on Anubis to appear in a bowl of rainwater. During the Greco-Roman period the depictions of Anubis changed somewhat. He became associated with the Greek goddess Hekate and god Hermes as psychopomps and underworld gods. He was seen as being in charge of legions of thousands of daemons, and could be appealed to for protection against malefic magic such as curses.

The red knotted threads used to bind supernatural enemies, which may be found in numerous folk traditions around the world, were known as *Anubis threads* in ancient Egypt, and were specifically linked to Anubis, as the god who binds and ties when he embalms, and when he controls daemons. Another use of knots was seen in the knotted red linen placed inside a woman's vagina to prevent miscarriage (found in the *London Medical Papyrus*).

It is clear that Anubis is one of the most enduring and multi-functional gods, an atavistic power from primeval times associated with birth and death, magic, protection, curses and demons. His role as the psychopomp enables him to travel between the worlds, and to act as guardian, a role later seen in the Christian church with St Christopher the Cynocephalus, showing his ability to even travel between pantheons. It is Anubis who instructs us appropriately in the *Pyramid Texts*: *"Anubis, foremost of the god's booth, has commanded that you descend as a star, as the morning god."*

APOLLO

Celeste Barnes

To this day, as the Light of the Greek pantheon, Apollo remains one of the most beloved by both gods and humans alike. As a deity of archery, art, knowledge, light, medicine, music, plague, sun, and of oracles, his domain is vast reaching. His influence and role in society is one of the most important in the world of the ancients Greeks. He also remains the only deity that, upon adoption into the Roman pantheon, kept his own name.

Born to Zeus and the Titaness Leto, Apollo's beginning was not peaceful. When it was discovered that Leto was with child, Hera began to relentlessly hunt the mother to be. In her fury, Hera refused to allow Leto to give birth on solid ground. Unable to find a safe place to give birth, Leto was driven from land to land. It was only after wandering around aimlessly, that she discovered a tiny Cycladic island. This island, which did not have a fixed position in the sea and was consistently being beaten by the waves and the winds, was the only one willing to accept her. Once Leto settled there, the island became fixed in place and was given the name Delos "The Unconcealed One" This would be where she would give birth to Artemis – goddess of the hunt and of the moon – who would then assist her twin, Apollo, into the world.

At only four days old, Apollo called upon his father to request a bow and arrows. Zeus honored this request and had a golden bow commissioned by Hephaestus. Once he had them in his possession, Apollo left Delos, setting out to avenge his mother. This took him to the mainland where he found Python, the chthonic dragon. Drawing his bow, he wounded Python. Injured, Python sought refuge in Delphi. There, Apollo was able to slay the beast.

Still furious, Hera sent the giant, Tityos, after Leto. Apollo and Artemis joined together to protect their mother. During the battle, Zeus provided aid and hurled Tityos deep into Tartarus. The twins again teamed up when Niobe claimed herself more superior to Leto because she had bared fourteen children compared to Leto's set of twins. Using poisoned arrows, Apollo killed Niobe's sons while Artemis killed her daughters with the silver bow that she had requested from their father.

There are many stories of how Apollo was given prophecy

and Delphi. Some state that he was given the gift of prophecy by dolphins, others say he learned it while he was working alongside mortals to redeem himself for the slaying of Python and was given Delphi by his grandmother, Phoebe. No matter how it began, the Oracle of Delphi became intimately connected with Apollo. Originally, the Oracle Pythia would channel him once yearly but this rapidly changed as word of the Oracle spread. Soon, many came to seek the counsel of Apollo with offerings of money, laurel leaves, or a black ram. Pythia's guidance was sought by Greek rulers before they made major decisions. Her words were highly respected, and sought, by those in Asia Minor, Egypt, and Rome as well.

Apollo's temples can still be found in Delphi in Greece, Pompeii in southern Italy, and The Temple of Apollo at Didyma in Miletus in modern day Turkey. Didyma was the fourth largest temple in the Greek world and housed another of Apollo's oracles. This oracle was second only to Delphi.

When it came to Apollo's appearance, he was considered to be one of the most beautiful with his hairless body, hair of gold and his eyes of blue. Much like the majority of deities, Apollo had many lovers most of which ended in tragedy. Apollo's love affairs reference both males and females, gods and humans. His most persistent courtship, that of the nymph Daphne, was never rewarded. Rather than submit to his desires, she transformed herself into a laurel tree. After that, the laurel tree became his sacred plant.

Medicine and healing have been attributed to Apollo whether it is through himself or mediated through his son, Asclepius, who was killed by Zeus after exploiting his healing by raising men from the dead. Though, Apollo is credited with many healings, he was also a god that could bring ill-health and plague as seen during the Trojan war when he and Artemis sided with the Trojans.

Apollo is often depicted with lyre in hand. The lyre was

a gift from a young Hermes after he stole several of Apollo's cattle. After the theft, upon locating Hermes, Apollo fell in love with the sound of the lyre. He exchanged the stolen cattle for the lyre.

Still relevant today, Apollo is calling out to those that would hear him. Ideas for connecting with him are: Taking up archery or a stringed instrument. Writing, singing, music are also sacred to this god of the arts. One can take up healing (whether a physical form or energy healing such a Reiki) or take up at least one form of divination.

ARTAOIS

Andrew Anderson

Artaois, also referred to as Artaius, and sometimes as Ardehe and Arthe, is a Celtic tribal God. While some believe he is named after the town Artaix, it is more commonly believed that he is a bear God. The name "Artaois" seems to derive from the Celtic word "Art", meaning bear, aligning him with the goddess Artio, a statue of whom can be found in the Swiss City of Bern. Artaois is referred to in a single Romano-Celtic inscription from the Isére region of eastern France, over the border from the cult of the bear goddess in Switzerland. The inscription reads "MERCVRIO AVG ARTAIO", or *"To the august Mercury Artaois"*, his name becoming an epithet to the God Mercury from the Roman pantheon. The practice of using the names of Celtic Gods as epithets was common during the Roman period, with Artaois being one of nearly three hundred deities remembered this way.

His association with Mercury has been used to suggest that Artaois was a god of financial success and plenty. It is interesting to note that Artaois was not aligned with the Roman God of war, Mars, a figure more frequently used in the Romano-Celtic alignment process. In many cultures, bears are clearly linked to ideas of warriorship and warfare, notably in Norse mythology where the berserker warriors take their name from "Ber", the Norse word for bear. Similarly, in Celtic culture, warriors were praised as being vigorous like a bear if they performed great feats. However, this connection purely to warriorship does not seem to be the case with Artaois. It is, however, believed he would have had a more general role as the embodiment of a successful tribal leader beyond simply being a God of financial success, combining the talents of a warrior, craftsman and magician. The suggestion of this comes from the development of the Bear Son legend, a common myth which underpins the development of many heroic leader figures around the globe, whether they be obviously connected to bears or not. In the tale of the Bear Sons, the progeny of a human mother and an immortal bear father become questing heroes and leaders, who undertake great feats and return to their society victorious. The Bear Son legend forms the basis for such literary figures as Odysseus and Beowulf.

Some believe that Artaois was a similar figure for his original worshippers in Isére and that his exploits, over time, merged with the stories of a tribal leader from Britain and formed the basis for the tales of King Arthur. This connection can be clearly seen in the "Art" morpheme within both names and in the belief that Arthur did not die but is waiting, hibernating like a bear, ready to return to protect his people in a messianic, Godlike way in their time of greatest need. Because of the connection to heroic figures, Artaois is generally depicted as a human male in a bearskin, rather than as a bear itself, reinforcing his connection to human society rather than to the natural world, which, in many cultures, tends to be the realm of the bear Goddess.

Although there is no explicit link in Celtic culture between Artaois and the stars, it is believed that the mythology surrounding the constellation Ursa Major dates from pre-historic times. Similarly, the constellation is linked to bear archetypes in cultures around the northern hemisphere. However, the Latin name, Ursa Major, also suggests that that the constellation is named after a She-bear. As an embodiment of the legendary Bear Son, Artaois should perhaps be more readily associated with the constellation Ursa Minor, or the small bear, separate but close to the more dominant female bear qualities, high in the sky looking down upon his followers. Artaois, like Arthur, seems to be in a phase of hibernation at the moment, only barely remembered within the historical record but with many in the world beginning to sense his influence again.

To honour Artaois today, many practitioners are trying to connect to the bear energy in Europe and in Britain. They support re-wilding and re-introduction projects which aim to bring the sacred presence of the bear back to these lands. Many also study the legends of Arthur, honouring not only the fantastic tales of chivalry and questing but, more importantly, the qualities of leadership which we need to learn from him in the twenty-first century. Working with the Wheel of the Year and aligning it with the yearly cycle of the bear is also an excellent way of channelling the energy of Artaois and honouring him in our lives. At a time of ecological peril, the re-emergence of the bear Gods, humanity's primal animal totem, should be of great significance and comfort for those who walk the path of nature religions.

ASCLEPIUS, GOD OF HEALING

Angela Paine

Asclepius the physician was originally a historical figure in ancient Greece. He was so skilful at healing the sick that after his death he was deified, also acquiring a God, Apollo, for a father. In the fifth century BCE Pindar's Pythian Ode describes Asclepius thus:

"To each for every various ill he made the remedy, and gave deliverance from pain, some with gentle songs of incantation; others he cured with soothing draughts of medicines, or wrapped their limbs around with doctored salves, and some he made whole with the surgeon's knife."

According to the myth that grew up around Asclepius, Apollo, his father, had intercourse with the nymph Coronis, a princess of Thessaly, and she became pregnant. Apollo ordered a white raven to guard her, while he left and went back to the land of the Gods, where she was forbidden to enter. Coronis fell in love with the mortal Ischys and had intercourse with him. When the watchful raven flew to Apollo to relate her unfaithful deed, the enraged Apollo scorched the feathers of the unfortunate bird with a fiery blast, turning him black from that day onwards. He then sent his sister, Artemis, to kill Coronis. She built a funeral pyre and flung Coronis onto it. Apollo watched, appalled as the mother of his unborn child was being consumed by the fire, then plunging a knife into Coronis in exactly the right place, he was able to deliver his son, whisking him away from the flames, unharmed.

According to a different myth Coronis gave birth to Asclepius and exposed him on Mount Titthion, where Apollo found him. He carried his newborn son to Chiron the centaur, who lived in a cave on mount Pelion, and asked him to bring him up. Chiron, the wounded healer, taught the young Asclepius everything he knew about the healing properties of the plants which grew on the mountain. He taught him surgery, aphrodisiacs and incantations and Asclepius grew up to become the best and most renowned physician in Greece, even able to cure snake bite, the most difficult ailment of all. After his death he was always depicted carrying a snake-entwined staff, an image that has been adopted by physicians throughout the world.

According to myth, Asclepius may have married Hygeia,

Goddess of cleanliness, or he may have married Epione, and Hygeia may have been his daughter. In ancient Greece, not only did men and women become Gods and Goddesses, but Gods and Goddesses became mortal, and/or married mortals. All Asclepius's children grew up to become physicians and healers, known as the Asclepiads. He had many sons, including Machaon and Podalirius, who helped Menelaos when he was wounded in the Trojan War. His daughter, Panacea was the Goddess of the cure-all remedy. The most famous doctor of the family was Hippocrates.

The Goddess Athena who had somehow acquired the blood of the Medusa, was so impressed by Asclepius's healing abilities that she gave him a present of some of this magical blood, telling him that it would restore life to the dead. On several occasions he used it, to the horror of Hades, God of the underworld, who was infuriated every time one of "his" dead souls returned to the world of the living. The dead, he thundered, belonged to him. He petitioned Zeus to put a stop to this iniquitous behaviour, so Zeus raised a thunderbolt and struck Asclepius dead. Zeus, like many fiery personalities, repented of his rash and hasty action, since Asclepius had been such a wonderful doctor. So, he turned him into the constellation Ophiochus, where he has remained ever since, shining down on us from the sky. Greek myth and Astrology are inextricably intertwined, many of the Gods and Goddesses also finding a place in the night sky, where they continue to govern our fate.

The myth of Asclepius is connected with the origins of medical science and the healing arts. After his death he became a God and people believed that he had the power to cure them, so they began to build temples, Asclepieion, to honour him. The temples were healing centres with sanctuaries to the God Asclepius and dormitories, where the sick were encouraged to sleep, surrounded by non-poisonous snakes which lived in the dormitories. Snakes were considered to be symbols of regeneration, since they shed their skins, and people thought that they brought luck and blessing to the sick. As the sick lay dreaming, the God Asclepius came to them and told them how to be cured. The patient then related their dream to the Asclepieion priest, who provided treatment and an explanation of the dream. The most famous Asclepieion were at Epidaurus and Kos, where visitors can still see the ruins of the healing centres.

JTN (ATEN)

Jennifer Uzzell

'Aten' is the term used in Egyptian inscriptions for the sun-disc; the physical, visible manifestation of the solar deities. In earlier times it was not viewed as a god in its own right. The first mention of Aten as a god is in the 12th Dynasty '*Story of Sinuhe*' where the murdered Pharaoh '*ascends to the heavens*' to merge with the Aten. It was not unusual for a dynasty to choose a patron deity and the 18th Dynasty associated itself particularly with solar deities with the Aten becoming increasingly important. Amenhotep III seems to have developed the cult of the Aten, using 'Tjekhen-Aten' (Radiance of the Aten) as one of his epithets.

It was, however, his son, Amenhotep IV, who took the worship of Aten to unprecedented levels. In the fifth year of his reign (c, 1347 BCE) he changed his name to Akhenaten or 'Essence/Life Force of the Aten'. This year also probably marks the start of construction work on a new city, Akhetaten (Horizon of Aten), which Akhenaten claimed to have been led to in a vision. In the seventh year of his reign, he moved the royal court away from Thebes and to this new capital. This move also freed him from the immediate influence of the priests of Amun in Thebes, with whom his family seem to have been in conflict for several generations.

Akhenaten developed the cult of Aten into what amounted

to a new religion over the years that followed. Scholars have referred to this as 'Atenism' and there has been much debate over whether it was monotheistic (acknowledging the existence of only one God) or henotheistic (allowing that the other gods existed but were subsidiary to Aten.) Images of other gods were banned and their priesthoods persecuted. The Aten was worshipped in temples open to the sun and no images of him were made. Instead, the royal family were depicted bathed in rays emanating from the sun disc, which terminated in hands giving blessing or in the ankh, a symbol of life.

It was this relationship with the royal family that made the new religion unique. Only they could worship Aten directly, all others derived life and blessing from worship of the Pharaoh and his family. It was he (Akhenaten) who operated the scales of justice and decided which of the dead would be allowed to live on in the afterlife. In his *Great Hymn to the Aten* he refers to himself as *'your son, who came from your body.... Whom you have taught your ways.'* However, Akhenaten appears to have become obsessed with his priestly role to the exclusion of matters of state leading to a decline in the fortunes of Egypt towards the end of his reign.

After his death, leaving an eight-year-old heir, the priesthood of Amun was quick to reassert its authority, changing the name of the new king from Tut-Ankh-Aten to Tut-Ankh-Amun ('The Living Image of Amun'). The name of Akhenaten and all references to Aten were removed from monuments and records and the deity fell back into obscurity.

BAAL

Laurie Martin-Gardner

For anyone familiar with the Hebrew Bible, Baal is an infamous name. The adversary of Yahweh, a multitude of Old Testament verses chronicle the war waged by Yahweh to turn his people away from the worship of the "false" Lord of the Earth. One prominent scene from the Book of First Kings chronicles 400 priests of Baal pitted against the prophet Elijah in a contest to prove which god, Baal or Yahweh, was the mightiest. When Elijah wins, he orders the priests slaughtered and their remains scattered. The biblical propaganda against Baal was quite effective and even today many still consider him a demon or even Satan himself. But the true Baal reigned as the Lord of Rain and Dew, the Rider of the Clouds, and the king of the Canaanite pantheon.

Much of what we know about Baal comes from a series of fragmented texts discovered in the ancient city of Ugarit known as the Baal Cycle. The son of the goddess Athirat (Asherah) and the God of Crops, Dagon (although some texts call him the son of El, the Supreme God of Canaan), Baal was the archetypal fertility god whose blessed rains allowed the grain to grow, the livestock to flourish, and the community to prosper. Much of the beginning has been lost, but the epic begins after an unknown dispute between Baal and El that results in El declaring the violent sea god, Yam, the King of the Gods. Unhappy with this decision and the harshness of his rule, Baal challenges Yam to a battle for supremacy. With the aid of two magical weapons, Baal defeats Yam and ascends the heavenly throne. Afterwards, with the intercession of Athirat, El grants Baal permission to have a palace built of cedar, gems and precious metals. From his sprawling home on Mount Saphon, Baal ruled as The Most High; using only the power of his words and voice to send forth the life giving rain to his people.

The story however, was far from over. The final part of the Baal Cycle introduces Mot, a personification of death and sterility. After being insulted by a dinner invitation from Baal, Mot threatens Baal and ultimately kills him. With Baal's death, the world begins to wilt. Without the Storm God's rains, nothing can grow and a terrible drought spreads throughout the land. Upon hearing that Baal has been killed, El enters a period of mourning. But Anath, Baal's sister and Goddess of War, is not content to simply mourn her beloved brother. Instead, she seeks revenge against Mot, eventually slaying him. Around the same time, El has a dream that Baal still lives. With the aid of Shapash, the Sun Goddess, the revived Baal returns to his throne and discovers that Mot too has been resurrected. The two battle again with no clear winner. In the end Mot, fearing punishment from El, admits defeat and declares that Baal is king.

Worship of Baal often occurred in "high places" alongside worship of his mother. Animal sacrifices and libations were offered to the god by priests who, the Hebrew Bible records, would dance around the altar in an ecstatic trance. In larger cities, formal temples were dedicated to the god and often included sexual rituals to ensure the fertility of the people and the land.

Despite their fervent hatred of Baal, much of his worship was integrated into Judaism as his role as the Almighty was absorbed by Yahweh. The book of First Kings stresses Yahweh's dominion over nature, especially the storm that had long been associated with Baal. The eighteenth chapter of Psalm describes Yahweh with the traditional language found in worship of Baal. Psalm 29 is borrowed almost word for word from an Ugaritic poem in honor of the Storm God. Psalm 89:25 has Yahweh declaring *"I will set his hand over the sea, his right hand over the rivers."* Sea and River were both titles of Baal's enemy Yam. Both Baal and Yahweh were credited with the slaying of the beast Leviathan and with leading Israel out of Egypt at the time of the Exodus.

Regardless of how much of Yahweh's identity once belonged to him, Baal was singled out by the Hebrews as a false god sent to lead the people astray. Again, and again the Hebrews reverted back to the traditional worship of Baal, much to the annoyance of the prophets and zealots. Evidence suggests that his importance did not wane until well after the period of the Babylonian exile in the 6th century BCE. Eventually, however, the Hebrews succeeded in destroying the cult of Baal and rewriting his story into one of deceit and evil. But thanks to discoveries such as those in Ugarit, the true Baal is finally being revealed.

BELENUS

Rachel Patterson

A few years ago, I visited the ancient city of Bath in Somerset, UK. There stands the Roman baths which are built over a natural hot spring. The site also hosts several nods to deity, mainly those of the ancient British goddess Sulis, later re-named Minerva by the Romans. But also, a strange 'gorgon' relief that some believe represents the god Belenus. I was quite taken with the image but thought little more of it until last year when he made himself known to me.

The gorgon head in the Roman baths depicts a male face with rays coming out in the form of hair and a beard. Some suggest these are snakes and that it is an image of Medusa, but I don't see it. The face is clearly male for a start, and the 'rays' are much more like hair than snakes. The image is in the temple that housed the sacred springs to Sulis. The Celtic word 'sul' means 'eye' or 'sun' and is the root of the goddess' Sulis' name. It makes sense to me to have a healing god at the baths along with the healing goddess. It could be an image of Apollo, but the Roman fashion was to be clean shaven. This image is much more along the lines of a hairy Celt!

The name appears in various spellings; Belenus, Belanos, Belanus, Belenos, Belin-us and Belus Bel. He is generally seen as a sun god with healing powers although little evidence suggests he was specifically a sun god originally. Perhaps due to his associations with fire, the fire festival of Beltane, healing and the Sun rays around his images, he has been thought of as such. However, he is believed to be a god of light, health and healing which often links him to healing waters, wells and springs. He is also associated with agriculture and specifically cattle.

Some suggestion is made that his name translates as 'the shining god'. Perhaps another link to the fire festival of Beltane. Beltane marks the beginning of summer and I do think this is Belenus' time of year, right through to Samhain. I have also seen suggestion that his name may be derived from the word 'belisa' which is the given name for the plant, henbane. It has a psychoactive affect, so perhaps it also gives a prophecy side to this god? The name may also have originated from the proto Celtic 'Guelenos' which has the meaning of 'source, well', could that be the healing spring connection?

He is one of the deities that is thought to traverse the sky in a horse drawn chariot. Bringing the sun with him or riding the sun in some stories. Artefacts have been found with this image and others where he is using a wheel as a shield or his face is surrounded by rays of light. Each one is thought to be the Celtic god Belenus.

The symbol of a horse recurs throughout, often in the shape of clay horses that were left as offerings. A coin found dating back to 1AD shows an image of a face with a moustache and hair spread out in rays, thought to be of Belenus. The reverse has an image of a wild boar, perhaps a suggestion to him being a warrior or his strength, or maybe just food!

I have also seen mention that Belenus had a consort, the Gaulish goddess Belisama. It does make some sense to me; she would suit him very well. Evidence has been found that a cult of Belenus covered Italy to Gaul including Britain, Ireland and Austria. Inscriptions to him can be found in France, Italy, Iberia and Britain.

Shrines to Belenus have been found in both Scotland and

France. The focus seems to be on healing and shrines for that purpose have also been found seemingly dedicated to dual gods, Belenus and Apollo. There does seem to be a similarity between the two.

The Welsh god Beli and Irish god Bile are also sometimes believed to be another incarnation of Belenus, not a theory I hold personally though. I think the attributes are too different between them. In Geoffrey of Monmouth's 'History of the Kings of Britain' he gives the name of Belinus as a King. Perhaps also originating from the god Belenus? The ancient British King, Cunobelinus deserves a mention, his name translated means 'hound of Belenus'.

Roman historians make reference to Belenus. Herodianosin in 278BCE tells of Roman soldiers seeing an image of the god Belenus in the sky, as a protector to them whilst in battle. 3rd Century Roman emperors Diocletian and Maximan made dedications to Belenus in Aquileia. Inscriptions to him have also been discovered at Altinium, Concordia and Lulium Carnicum.

He definitely had a large following and does appear to have been widely worshipped. For me, personally, I see him as a healing god, not particularly on the physical side but more along the lines of spiritual and mental healing. He is strength, power, support and guidance. I do like to think of him as a sun god, that fits nicely for me. Using his power from Beltane to Samhain when he is at his full strength. Whatever you choose to believe he is an interesting deity to work with.

BES

Emily Guenther

Bes is a unique deity from Ancient Egypt whose worship is gaining popularity with some modern Pagans. Bes' origins are lost in history, but in one form or another, he was worshipped by the Ancient Egyptians since Old Kingdom times (2686–2181 BCE). Bes is the Ancient Egyptian demon-queller, protector of the home, women, children and childbirth.

The god whom we now know as Bes may have begun as a variety of other protector deities who were all eventually assimilated into the dwarf-lion Bes. Other dwarf deities with very similar natures to that of Bes include Aha, who was the earliest incarnation of the dwarf god, and the god Hayet. Appearing in the Middle Kingdom (2055 BCE–1650 BCE), Aha was a war-like god who was depicted face-on with legs bent, wearing a lion mask and tail, and holding snakes. Hayet was an exorcist who warded off demonic spirits, especially through dance. He was characterized by having a beard, a crown with five tall feathers, a lion tail and a belt. Other deities, called Tetetenu, Kherau, Amam, Mefdjet and Menew were also associated with, and could be merged with, the dwarf god Bes. Most of these names are related to violence, such as strife, fighting, lamenting, et cetera.

The Ancient Egyptians believed that life and the world was filled with dangers and demons. Demons could take various guises in Ancient Egypt, therefore one had to be sure to live purely and truthfully, and to also be aware of their environments. The idea that gods such as Bes were there to protect people from not only supernatural dangers, but also mundane dangers such as snakes and crocodiles, must have brought great comfort to the people of Ancient Egypt.

Bes is portrayed as a dwarf god with leonine features. He has short legs, an enlarged head with a beard and a protruding tongue. Bes is often shown with a lion's mane, lion's tale or wearing the skin of a lion. Sometimes Bes is shown with a large belly and breasts, perhaps to indicate his protection over pregnant women. In his hands he carries the tools of his trade. Images of Bes show him carrying rattles and other musical instruments that he would use to scare away demons, intent upon causing harm. Some images show Bes carrying an infant, knives or other weapons, or the hieroglyph "sa" which means protection. The "sa" symbol was carried by both Bes and his wife Taweret, the hippopotamus goddess of childbirth and protection, and was used as an amulet by the Ancient Egyptians. Bes is one of only two Ancient Egyptian deities portrayed fully facing the observer. Most Egyptian deities are portrayed in profile. The other deity shown face forward is Hathor. Hathor and Bes share connections through their protection, love of music and dance, and the fact that both deities are thought to have originated outside of the land of Egypt.

In his role as protector of women, children and childbirth, Bes' image was carved or painted on furniture and walls in nurseries or birthing houses. In fact, Bes is one of the few gods that artifacts show was popular with the common people of Ancient Egypt. The Egyptians also saw Bes as one who not only protected but entertained children. When a child smiled for no reason, it was thought that Bes was pulling faces at the child to make them laugh. He is thought to entertain through dancing and singing, and so he was also thought to be a god of happiness and joviality. Bes uses dancing and singing to both entertain children and scare away demons and danger.

It was during the Greek Period (332–30 BCE) that the worship of Bes became widespread. The numbers of amulets and charms, as well as reliefs at the temples show how popular the 'Great Dwarf' god became. There were even oracles of Bes, to whom the people would ask questions of, written on papyrus.

Bes had no temples and no priesthood other than his oracle, although he was a major deity at Khemenu during the Middle Kingdom (2055 BCE–1650 BCE). Later in Egyptian history, statues and depictions of Bes were found in most homes throughout the land of Egypt. Although not originally one of the more famous of the gods, Bes came to be loved by the people of Egypt. It was the dwarf god-demon Bes that they came to call on for protection in their daily lives.

Modern Pagans who wish to connect with Bes may consider inviting him into their homes and asking him to help protect it. Singing, dancing, and making merry are also ways to connect with Bes and honor him. Handmade crafts made in his image or honor are also well received by the jovial yet fierce god.

BRAGI

Susan baker

Bragi is widely recognised as a member of the Æsir, the Norse God of Poetry and the Patron God of Skalds (Poets). It is unclear whether Bragi as a God and member of the Æsir truly existed before the ninth century AD when a highly talented (human) Norwegian poet, Bragi Boddason, was recorded as serving multiple Swedish Kings before his death. The most notable of these Kings were Ragnar Loðbrok, Östen Beli and Björn at Hauge. This is because there are no currently discovered surviving written records that have Bragi's name in them before this time. It is possible that upon his death, such a talented person was deified by those who knew of his talents, and over time his name was added to the lists of Æsir. It is also possible that due to Bragi Boddason's talents more people were made aware of the God Bragi and as such the God received an increase in worship, reverence and, most importantly, documentation. Whichever is the truth, Bragi is now widely known as the God of Poetry and the premier Skald within the Æsir.

There is another uncertainty regarding the God Bragi, and that about his mother. The general consensus is that his father was Odin, but who his mother was is a little murkier. This could be due to many factors, such as his later addition to the Æsir suggested by the above or tales about him from different tribes, clans and kingdoms having different origins for him and only the most common surviving to be recorded in history. Whichever it is, the two most common options given for his mother are Frigga, Odin's wife, or Gunnlod, a giantess and daughter of Suttung, the giant who guarded the Sacred Mead. As there is a recorded story describing how Odin gained the Sacred Mead that has Gunnlod conceiving and birthing a child that fits Bragi's description, and no such surviving story between Odin and Frigga, it is easier to accept that Bragi is the child of Odin and Gunnlod and through them, is half Æsir and half giant. This would also explain his acceptance in the Æsir as well as Frigga's dismissal of him in *Lokasenna*.

What we do know for certain, is that Bragi is one of very few of the Æsir or Vanir who is welcome no matter which realm he finds himself to be in and was also one of the few non-warrior Gods within the Æsir. This can be seen in his lack of weapon or other war-related object as a symbol. Rather his symbol is that of a harp. Differing stories about him have the Dwarves gifting Bragi with a golden harp.

Whilst Bragi is the Patron of Skalds, Poets, Bards as well as eloquence and all those who use words to express their inner fire and creativity, there are no known cults attached to him. This is notable because of the importance that Norse and Germanic cultures of the time put on poetry, both the telling and creating of it. If your deeds weren't great enough to be recorded for posterity in poetry or song, you wouldn't be remembered and would likely not reach Valhalla or any other great hall for the dead. Also because of this lack of cult surrounding Bragi, there are no known holy days for him, nor any recorded structure of how or when to worship him, dedicate anything to him or the like. The closest to this is that Skalds of both sexes were also known as Braga-men or Braga-women.

Suppositions on how and when to worship Bragi can be made from the things he is God of; Poets, Bards, Skalds and those who express themselves and pass on information through word and tune. As such, here are a few ideas of how to worship him:

- Dedicate all of your poetry, song and creative writing to him
- Honour him with your performances of the same
- Make time in your days to learn new techniques, memorise poems/sagas/songs etc.

When to worship him is a little trickier and there seems to be no consensus. Certainly, you could call upon him when you have a performance to give. Or you could dedicate it to him.

As well as these, you should also act with honour to your fellow people and dedication to your craft. Why? Well, how else are you to go down in history as someone to be remembered? An honourable person who did the most with their talents and used them to bring cheer and spread information within their people is far more likely to be remembered, even if their works aren't published (at least not in the conventional manner) than someone who thought about writing something at some time who was an OK person to some.

BRAN

Melusine Draco

Bran is one of the few truly British gods who can trace his ancestry to pre-Celtic times. Usually referred to as 'Bran the Blessed' or Bran Fendigaidd in Welsh, that literally means 'blessed crow or raven'. He was a legendary King of Britain and a fearless warrior; a popular figure in the bardic traditions and well-known in Welsh mythology during the Iron Age.

Legend describes him as a giant of semi-divine heritage who possessed supernatural strength and abilities. His father was Llyr, the god of the sea; and he was also brother to Branwen, of whom he was fiercely protective – playing his most significant role in the *Mabinogi: Branwen ferch Llyr*. A patron of poetry and music, Bran was hailed as the personification of sovereignty, eventually being venerated as a god, a hero and a powerful king among the numerous tribes of Britain where he was associated with ravens as a god of prophecy.

Ravens and crows were revered in the ancient world as they were thought to be messengers between this and the Otherworld and black ravens came to symbolise the presence of Brân and were sacred to him. This belief has persisted and Corvidae are still considered to be messengers from the Otherworld amongst traditional witches. Similarly, the alder tree was associated with Brân because his warriors used a dye made from alder trees to paint their faces red.

In some of the older myths, Llyr was a god of the sun of the Coritani tribe, who married the sea goddess Iwerydd, from a god-like race called the Tuatha De Danann in Ireland and their offspring were Bran and Branwen. A second marriage took place between Llyr and a noblewoman called Penarddun from the Belgae tribe and other siblings were born from the union.

The most famous legend about Bran ap Llyr began when he was the most powerful chieftain in Britain, living with his family at their home in Harlech on the Welsh coast. The Irish king Matholwch asked for the hand of his sister Branwen in marriage in order to forge an alliance between the two islands but the celebrations are cut short when Efnisien, a half-brother to the pair, mutilated Matholwch's horses, angry that his permission was not sought in regards to the marriage. Matholwch was deeply offended until Bran offered him compensation in the form of a magic cauldron that could restore the dead to life. Pacified by the valuable gift, Matholwch and Branwen sailed to Ireland.

Once Branwen had given birth to a son, Gwern, she was mistreated, banished to the kitchens and beaten every day. She tamed a starling and sent it across the sea with a message to her brother, who sailed from Wales to rescue her with a host of warriors. The Irish offered to make peace but secretly plotted to kill their guests during a feast; Efnisien, suspecting a trick, foiled the plot but again taking offence throws his young nephew Gwern on the fire and a savage battle breaks out. Discovering that Matholwch had been using the cauldron to revive their dead, Efnisien hid among the corpses and destroyed the cauldron, sacrificing himself in the process since living bodies could not be placed in the magic vessel.

Matholwch's mistreatment of the British princess led to a mutually destructive war, resulting in the deaths of most of the principal characters. Only seven warriors survived the conflict – Branwen having died of a broken heart – and were told by the mortally wounded Bran to cut off his head and to return it to Britain. The warriors finally reached Caer Lludd or modern-day London, where they buried his head on the site of the White Hill – where the White Tower now stands. As long as it remained there, Britain would be safe from invasion, since Bran was regarded as Britain's protector who had willingly sacrificed himself to keep the island safe from invasion. However, King Arthur later dug up the head, declaring the country would be protected only by *his* great strength and as a result Britain suffered the humiliation of the subsequent Roman and Norman invasions.

The cauldron was an everyday implement in the home and yet it appears in many variations of the across Europe where every important element in the rural economy took on religious significance. It was seen as a means of transformation, for it changed the inedible into the edible; it was a life-giver and was an aspect of the Great Cauldron of the gods – particularly in Britain as a reminder of the divine pre-Celtic hero, Bran.

Today we rarely encounter him outside traditional Welsh literature but he deserves his place among those who follow the Old Ways as a symbol of faith and honour and possibly Britain's greatest hero.

BRES

Sue Perryman

The tale of Bres appears in the Lebor Gabàla, the Irish book of Invasions. The stories within the Lebor Gabàla hold only a memory of the original tales which would have been passed on through word of mouth over generations and embellished with each re-telling. Much of Irish mythology was written by Christian monks who added their own slant, the gods became kings, heroes and Fairies, could Bres have originally been an agricultural god as some believe?

The origins of the Tuatha De Danann and how they arrived in Ireland change depending on your source, but what is clear is that they were skilled in magic, science and the arts. Some say they sailed to Ireland, led by their King Nuada and upon landing burned their boats so they could not escape from the Fir Bolg who ruled the land.

The first battle of Mag Tuired was fought, and although the Tuatha De Danann defeated the Fir Bolg, Nuada's arm was cut off. The God of physicians, Dian Chet made a replacement arm from silver, but Nuada was forced to abdicate as their law stated that only a physically perfect man could be king. To appease another tribe, the fierce Formorians, the Tuatha De Danann made an error in their choice of new king, they chose Bres, whose Father was Formorian and mother one of the Tuatha De Danann on the condition that if he did anything to displease them, he would abdicate.

Bres, also known as Eochaid Bres, is described as beautiful but harsh and inhospitable. Some versions of his story say he was married to the goddess Brigid, which suggests she may have originally been a sovereignty goddess who represented the land and legitimised a king by marrying and/or having sex with him.

Bres soon went back on his promise to the Tuatha De

Danann, forcing them to pay tribute to the Formorians and become their slaves. In time, Nuada's arm was healed by Miach, the son of Dian Cecht and his sister Airmid which gave the Tuatha De Danann hope and encouraged them to rise up and rebel against Bres and the Formorians. Bres fled to his father Elatha, demanding an army to destroy the Tuatha De Danann. Elatha refused to help him and advised Bres to seek help from another Formorian lord, Balor, who had a huge deadly eye that destroyed anything upon which it gazed.

With the support of Balor, Bres led the Formorians into the second battle of Mag Tuired. As the battle raged, a warrior pointed out to Bres that whenever a Tuatha De Danann warrior was killed they would be carried from the field, only to return alive and well shortly after, and when their weapons were damaged, they too would return intact. Bres called for his son Ruadan and ordered him to find out what was happening to the weapons. He then summoned the warrior Ochtriallach and ordered him to find out how the warriors were healed.

Ruadan disguised himself and searched until he came across Giobhniu, the God of smith's, Luchtaine, the god of carpenters and Credne, God of bronze workers standing beside a forge. As each broken weapon was handed to them, they magically repaired it. Ruadan made his way back to his father and told him what he had seen. Bres was furious and ordered Ruadan to kill Giobhniu. When Ochtriallach returned he explained that he had seen Dian Chet standing beside a well with his children chanting spells. They would plunge the slain warriors into the well before pulling them out alive. Again, Bres was incensed and ordered Ochtriallach to destroy the well.

Ruadan returned to the forge and asked Giobhniu for a spear, but as Giobhniu handed one to him Ruadan plunged it into Giobhniu's body. Seemingly fatally wounded, Giobhniu pulled the spear out and threw it back at Ruadan, the young man managed to crawl back to his father, dying at his feet. It is said that his mother Brigid wept and mourned so loudly that her grief became the first form of keening heard in Ireland. Meanwhile, Giobhniu crawled to the well where Dian Chet immersed him in the water which brought him back to life.

That night Ochtriallach and a band of Formorian warriors crept to the magical well and filled it with stones. The following day as battle commenced there were many casualties on both sides. Bres called for his champion, Balor, who killed Nuada, but the Tuatha De Danann hero Lugh Làmfada cast a stone from a slingshot into Balor's terrible eye, that went through his brain killing him. As Balor fell, he crushed many of his fellow warriors. Without their champion, the Formorians were soon overpowered, Lugh then found Bres trying to flee the battlefield, Bres begged for mercy and after much discussion he agreed to teach the Tuatha De Danann agriculture in exchange for his life.

CERNUNNOS

Mabh Savage

The cavalcade of fairy folk
Cernunnos in his winter cloak
Who calls to beasts; the stag, the hound
Who calls the great hunt, starts the sound
Of hooves a-drumming on the ground
Hide so you won't be found!
The green that rests within the oak
The holly still in winter's choke
Frantic, bursting to be free
Herne rides the land and sea.
(Mabh Savage, 2018)

Cernunnos is possibly one of the better known gods in modern and neo-paganism. The archetypal image of the horned god is particularly potent in religions such as Wicca. The horned god is often seen as the consort to the goddess, both her son and lover at differing points in the cycle of her story, and a symbol of death and rebirth.

Despite this well-known nature of the horned god, though, Cernunnos is oddly elusive. There is a distinct lack of any mention of this god throughout ancient literature, and evidence for his existence as a Celtic deity appears primarily on Celtic artefacts. The most famous of these is probably the Gundestrup Cauldron. This exciting and significant silver bowl was discovered in Denmark, and may date from as early as 200 BCE. The cauldron is heavily decorated outside and in. One of the interior plates shows a horned man, surrounded by animals. He holds a snake or serpent tightly, perhaps signifying his power over creatures or a protective nature; a deity who might keep harmful creatures at bay. Many of the other animals are facing him, as if in awe or because they want to come close to him. The god is cross-legged, at ease and calm. In his other hand he holds a torque, possibly signifying some sort of authority. A similar adornment is around his neck. Most notably, however, he has antlers. Antlers which are clearly and deliberately almost completely identical to those of the stag which stands to the left of him, but one prong shorter. The god carries the aspect of the stag: a creature that understand the forests, conflict, the rut, and what is feel like to be hunted.

There is some contention as to what the horns signify and the nature of this god which we now call Cernunnos. Some speculate that the "shamanic" pose on the Gundestrup cauldron indicates a peaceful nature, in harmony with nature and the wild animals. Others suggest that the horns or antlers point towards a more aggressive nature, and stronger links towards fertility and sexuality.

There is an interesting sculpture from France which may possibly be Cernunnos, thought so because of the torque around his neck and in his hands, and the fact that he is encircled by serpents who have ram's heads. This statue has three faces. This type of iconography often indicates that a deity has multiple facets or aspects. This would mean that Cernunnos is not simply peaceful, or aggressive, or sexual in nature. He may be, and may always have been, connected with all these aspects and perhaps many more.

Many attempts have been made to link Cernunnos to figures within Celtic literature. One conjecture is that Cernunnos may have been, or been connected to, Conall Cernach, a character from the Ulster Cycle of myths. This supposition is based on a tale called Táin Bó Fraích, The Cattle Raid on Fraech, in which a terrifying serpent is tamed by Conall, becoming the girdle around his waist, just like on the aforementioned statue from France.

Another potential link is to the Roman god Dis Pater or Dis, the god of the underworld. In medieval iconography, serpents were linked to the underworld, which could have made Cernunnos a god of life, nature, and death. This would certainly back up the modern use of him as a god of the seasons and rebirth. However, Dis has also been linked to Taranis, the Gaulish sky god, Donn, and Irish god of the dead and Beli Mawr from Welsh mythology.

We may never know what the true significance of Cernunnos was to our ancestors. I've only scratched the surface in this chapter, and the more scholars dig into the possible meanings of the rare pieces of evidence we have, the more questions seem to arise. What we can say, for certain, is that today Cernunnos has become a vital part of modern Pagan culture. He is occasionally linked with Herne, the hunter from British folk legend, and so the circle of hunter and hunted is complete.

Cernunnos reminds us of our links to nature, and that we are a part of nature, so to disrespect the natural world is to disrespect ourselves. He is the hibernating mammal in winter, the green buds in spring, the thriving forest in summer and the mice that run from the combine harvester during early autumn. He is every creature from the smallest to the most massive; from woodlouse to whale. And, as a primal, fertile god, he is the embodiment of love, sex, and creativity- which needn't be limited by gender or sexuality. Indeed, fertility can also be representative of ideas, projects, goals; anything which encourages growth and change.

Whether hunter or hunted, peaceful or powerful or both, Cernunnos is a vital part of modern Paganism and no matter our understanding of his ancient nature, his crucial role in contemporary duotheism and polytheism cannot be denied.

DIONYSUS

Ngatina C. Sylvanius

God in the vines, crowned with twisted ivy. God in the rising sap and fermenting wine, dance with me through the mountains. Speak through chants and swirling ecstasy, inspiring words enough to describe the complexity....

As early as the 13th century BCE the name of Dionysus was being spoken amongst the Mycenaeans and while, in later years, he has come to be misunderstood as simply a hedonist, this multi-dimensional deity has ancient beginnings and deep importance.

His creation is one of the more convoluted tales of Hellenic mythology; the son of Persephone, he was vengefully killed whilst still an infant – dismembered and eaten by the Titans. He was almost destroyed before he could even begin. However, the infant's heart was saved, allowing Zeus to use it to impregnate his mortal lover, Semele. Hearing how her husband was once more straying, Hera disguised herself as a crone and befriended

Semele. In this way she could encourage the pregnant girl to confront her lover and ask the god to reveal himself in his true form – that of a lightning bolt – killing the young mother instantly. Hera had not foreseen her husband's devotion to the unborn child and her revenge was frustrated by Zeus rescuing the developing Dionysus from the ashes of his mother. Unwilling to trust the continued gestation to anyone else, Zeus sewed the foetus into his thigh where Dionysus remained until he was ready to be re-born. After this second birth, Zeus sent the infant Dionysus to be raised by rain-nymphs in Nysa, a mythological land thought to be located in northern Africa. It was here that the young god learned the secrets of cultivating the grape vine and transforming its fruit into wine.

Dionysus was not safe from Hera just by virtue of having survived his childhood and eventually the jealous Queen of Mount Olympus found him. Rather than attempt yet again to kill him, she cursed him with amnesia and a wandering madness. This illness led him to travel widely before being found and cured in Phrygia (Turkey) by Cybele who also took him under her wing and trained him in her ritual forms. From here he travelled Asia, concentrating especially on India, spreading his worship and the knowledge of the vine, before making his way back to Greece.

Due to his complicated genesis, Dionysus was blessed with many attributes which reflect his history; a reincarnated god of vegetation, fruitfulness and wine, he also presided over vast celebrations (Dionysia) and accompanying performance arts. This is then taken further by his close association with drunkenness, ecstasy, orgiastic rites and madness. One of the main aspects of His worship was in the form of a Mystery Cult. The devotees were typically (although not always) women known as *Maenads* and the cult was both secretive and controversial in its practices. While the very nature of the cult means that little definitive is known about their practices, some aspects were common knowledge and were therefore recorded. Rites of the Maenads were held in rural areas, especially wooded mountains. In the evening groups robed in fawn skins would thread their way into the wilderness carrying torches, handheld drums (*tympanon*), double pipes (*aulos*), ritual staves tipped with pinecones (*thyrsus*) and of course, wine. Once the procession reached their destination, it is likely that they participated in rites including a type of ecstatic dancing to rhythmic music which is known as *oreibasia*. This dancing was purported to transport the initiates into a trance state in which, through their connection to the god, they gained unnatural strength and speed and were therefore able to hunt, capture and kill wild animals with their bare hands.

Of course, given Dionysus' patronage of the arts, creative renditions of these Maenads, and indeed the god himself, were produced and provide much of the surviving information about their perceived traits and practices. These depictions include the women suckling wild animals and also tearing such creatures apart and eating their raw flesh in the rite of *omophagia*. One of the most famous works is Euripides' tragedy 'The Bacchae' (405BCE), in which Pentheus, King of Thebes attempts to ban the practices of the mystery cult. He is subsequently torn to pieces by a group of entranced initiates including his own mother. This image reflects the understanding that many of the men who disapproved of the rites were punished harshly by Dionysus with dismemberment and insanity featuring highly in a reflection of the trials endured by the god Himself.

Over the years, many people focused on the connections to wine and ecstatic celebration and this led many to discount the god as a light-hearted 'party animal' when in reality he was considered bestial, but in a way more closely related to fertility and the complex mystery of nature.

EL

Laurie Martin-Gardner

Once believed to be little more than a synonym for "god", a chance discovery in the ancient city of Ugarit (present day Ras Shamra, Syria) in 1928, reintroduced the powerful Canaanite supreme god to the modern world. El was not simply "a god," but *the* god. Frequently portrayed as an older man with a long gray beard, El was the progenitor of gods and men, the Creator Eternal, the God of Wisdom, the Bull God of immense strength and uncommon compassion.

Although consort of the great mother goddess Athirat (Asherah) and father to over seventy deities, El is surprisingly absent from many of the surviving Canaanite myths. The first major text concerning El picks up sometime after the world has been created. In *Shachar and Shalim*, or *The Birth of the Gracious Gods*, El lives alone *"at the source of the double river, midst the upspringings of the deeps"* which supply the world with both sweet and salt waters. Walking along the sea shore, he encounters two women, the goddesses Athirat and Rahmayyu that present him with an offering. They cry out to him in a way that suggests they are performing a fertility ritual, and to impress them with his strength and prowess, El hurls his staff into the sky and kills a bird. Once the bird is roasting, he tells the women to make a choice. If they call him father, he will embrace them as his daughters. But if they call him husband, he will take them as his brides. The women call him husband and in time give birth to twins – Shachar and Shalim, Dawn and Dusk.

Despite being keenly aware of the sufferings of humanity and the exploits of the gods, El typically remained withdrawn and separate from his creations. Often other deities, particularly Athirat, would act as mediators between El and his people. A text that makes up part of the Baal Cycle of Ugaritic myths recalls an instance where Athirat is sent to El by her son Baal, the Storm God, who seeks permission from the great god to build his own mansion. It is not only gods that seek the blessings of El, however, and Athirat often beseeches her husband on the behalf of worthy mortal men as well. Slow to anger and quick to forgive, El rightfully earned the epithet of "The God of Mercy."

One very poignant scene in the Baal Cycle portrays a very different side of the Supreme God. When he learns that Baal is dead, El spirals quickly into despair. In his grief, El descends from his throne and throws himself on the ground. He puts aside his soft garments for sackcloth, covers his head in dust, and gashes his body with a stone. His songs of lamentation do not end until he has a vision that Baal is not dead. Only then does he rise and with joy in his voice declare that Baal lives. El may have been the creator of the universe, but he was also a father who loved deeply and mourned openly – qualities not often seen in the supreme gods of the ancient world.

No temples dedicated to the Bull God have ever been unearthed, but his name is prominent on surviving lists of sacrificial offerings. This may be because he was worshiped primarily in tents in the wilderness like the one he and his family withdrew to for eight years after the birth of Shachar and Shalim. Despite this, numerous bull icons believed to have been used in the worship of El have been unearthed along with inscriptions and hymns written in his honor. He may have been a distant god, but his presence was felt throughout the Canaanite world.

The Ugaritic texts undoubtedly added new dimension to a mostly forgotten god, but it is possible that he was actually hidden in a very prominent place – the Hebrew Bible. Most scholars now believe that the god of Genesis was not Yahweh, the god of the Israelites, but the Canaanite El instead. The similarities between the Ugaritic El and the Hebrew El are staggering. The language used to describe and pray to the gods are the same, the rituals are almost identical, and the Hebrew god is often referred to as El, Elohim, or other variations of the name. In Psalm 82, Yahweh stands among a council of gods and renders judgment against them, just as El had once done in Canaan.

Eventually El would be replaced by the younger god, Baal. But his importance would never be overshadowed, and he was always regarded as the Supreme God of Canaan. As the likely god of Abraham, echoes of El's influence can still be felt today.

EWICHER YEEGER

Cassandra Nilson

Ewicher Yeeger, to those of Urglaawe faith, is an earth-bound deity. In the myths of the Pennsylvania Dutch, he is known for having saved the people who settled farms around the Blobarrick from starvation. Using his hounds to drive game to the land the farmers had stripped bare.

The story goes that by 1732, German colonists had migrated to Pennsylvania. The colonists stripped the land of all trees and plants, and built their farms along the Blobarrick, or the Blue Mountain. The migrants brought with them their traditions, farming methods and way of life, but what they could not bring with them was their home climate. The colonists experienced a major drought. When the rain did come, it washed away the dry soil, including many of the seeds and the few seedlings that managed to take root. The drought was followed by a crop failure. Snowstorms made hunting parties impossible, and the local land stripped of its woods yielded no game.

The colonists became increasingly desperate and began to pray to whoever would listen and to set out what meagre offerings of hay and cloth they had. Though small, the offering would have cost them dearly, which in truth is the purpose of sacrifice. Just as sickness and starvation began to set in, the mid-autumn night's serenity was shattered by an overwhelming sound of barking hounds. The noise seemed to come from nowhere yet from all directions at the same time. The sound appeared intermittently throughout the dark of night while the colonists remained in their homes, frightened by the enormity of the noise.

As dawn approached, the settlers came out of their homes. They looked out onto the barren fields and saw that the wildlife had been driven back into the land. With deer and rabbit suddenly plentiful, the farmers took to hunting and to preserving the meat for the winter. Throughout that winter, the sound of the hunting pack could be heard across the Blobarrick. The magnitude of the sound never lessened, and the folk knew that they had been rescued them from certain starvation. The honoring and worship of Ewicher Yeeger (The Eternal Hunter) had begun.

When Ewicher Yeeger is depicted, he is generally seen as horned or antlered, with his hounds surrounding him. He is likened to Herne the Hunter, and the association is strong enough for some people to refer to Ewicher Yeeger as Hern. Some view the pre-thunder rumble of the sky as the baying of his hounds. This is not viewed in Urglaawe belief as the literal presence of the deity, rather the phenomena are seen as a time to remember and honor the god. A good way to do this is to light a candle near a window when the rumble begins. If you live in a storm prone area it's also a good start to a protection rite.

Ewicher Yeeger is said to be of the Wane (Vanir) and is seen as the consort of Holle. Within the lore of Continental Germany, Holle's consort is said to be either Holler, Wodan or Dunnor, depending on region. Urglaawe places him as part of the Wane due to his entirely earthbound nature. He is claimed to be of the Wild Hunt, but if so, it is in a secondary role. Apart from a handful of imagery depicting him in a hunt like setting, there is scant information to label these scenes "the wild hunt". Where he is tied to the Continental Germanic god Holler, he travels the woods collecting the weaker forest spirits who would not have survived the hunt. Many of Urglaawe faith believe the Butzlemann (a scarecrow type of effigy that guards the fields) burned at Allewiezle (a festive period roughly the same time and with similar tones to All Hallows) join with him to do battle and hold back the malevolent frost giants.

The motives of Ewicher Yeeger are said to be unknowable, or incomprehensible to humans. He is concerned primarily with the cycle of life and rebirth and can be benevolent to humans when their gain serves his purposes. While he can be compassionate, he can also be cruel, being more concerned with the wellbeing of the earth than us humans.

Ewicher Yeeger is seen as a woodland figure, directing game toward or away from humans as suits his mood. Both Germanic Holler and Scandinavian Ullr are attested as hunters, with Ullr's hall being named after his bow wood, Ydalir (Yew's Dale). Ullr is called upon when brute strength and unrelenting force is required. Holler, as the gentle god of winter and death, is called upon for terminations and transformations. With both of these connections, Ewicher is called upon whenever human efforts or resources are not quite enough. When everything else has been tried he hears the pleas. He can be called upon when you are truly in need, as the strong stoic father of the woods.

FINNBHEARA – FAIRY KING OF CONNACHT

Morgan Daimler

We have more named Fairy Queens than Kings but we do have a few examples of named Kings as well. In Ireland one of the most well-known of the Fairy Kings is Finnbheara, whose name may appear under different spellings including Finvara, Finveara, Fionbheara, Fin Bheara, Fionnbharr or Findbharr. In older Irish his name may be understood as 'Fair Haired'. Dáithí O hÓgáin connects the name to the summit of Cnoc Meadha and the cairn found there which are both associated with Finnbheara. In the Altram Tige Dá Medar he is called Finnbarr Meadha, or Finnbheara of Meadha.

His fairy hill is at Cnoc Mheada in county Galway and he is known as the king of the fairies of Connacht. He also has a strong connection to the dead and in some folklore is called the King of the Dead. The relationship between the fairies and the dead is complicated but we also see this sort of crossover with Donn Firinne, who is called both a Fairy King and a god of the dead. We shouldn't conflate the two groups entirely but this may indicate that Finnbheara has a chthonic nature.

Finnbheara is described as one of Tuatha De Danann, the old Gods of Ireland, in the Agallamh na Seanoach. In the Altram Tige Dá Medar we learn that he is the youngest son of the Dagda and a brother to Oengus mac ind Óg, connecting him to two very powerful members of the Tuatha De Danann. His mother is unknown. He is sometimes said to be a rival of another Fairy King, Donn Firinne. Ó hOgáin suggests that the two rival kings might symbolize complementary rulers of the year. Whether this is so or not Finnbheara certainly had a place among the Tuatha De Danann at one point in time and his importance was later shifted to his role as a king of the fairies.

Physical descriptions of Finnbheara are rare but the meaning of his name would indicate that he is fair haired. He is considered a handsome man, often described wearing black. Beyond these few details we could only surmise but anecdotal accounts would indicate an attractive and imposing figure.

Finnbheara has an infamous love of mortal women, despite his wife Una being described as incomparably beautiful. There are many anecdotal tales of him taking mortal women into his fairy hill, sometimes temporarily sometimes permanently. In one story he brings a woman named Eithne into Cnoc Meadha; after a year her husband manages to retrieve her by digging into the hill, salting the hole he created, and removing the fairy clothing Eithne had on which broke the enchantment holding her. In the Feis Tighe Chonain he is described as a rival with Finn mac Cumhal for the same woman.

He is often associated with horses, both broadly and specifically with horse racing. In one tale he appeared acting as jockey riding the horse of a human Lord in a race, to help that human win, before disappearing. In another story he is riding a black horse and in a different account he appears in a coach drawn by four white horses.

Finnbheara is known to take people for various purposes but also to bless humans sometimes without obvious reason. He will reward any blacksmith willing engage in the dangerous venture of shoeing his three-legged horse, and in one account when a sick woman gave him some bread, he healed her illness. He will appear to humans and offer them his help if it suits him, particularly in horse racing, and in some instances, he invites humans into his fairy hill. While some of these may be cases of Finnbheara taking people forever in others the person is simply a guest and would be allowed to leave freely. In several stories where humans find themselves feasting with Finnbheara the other guests are dead people they knew in life.

The success of crops in Connacht are said to rest on Finnbheara's presence there and his good will. In some anecdotal accounts the crops flourish when Finnbheara and his fairies win in contests against rival groups of fairies. There was a standing rivalry between Finnbheara's fairies in Connacht and the fairies in Ulster, with the two groups often fighting. In one anecdote the fairies of Ulster and Connacht met as clouds in the air and fought and *"it was thought that Finnbheara won because there were good crops in Connacht that year."*

Finnbheara is a complex and important figure, a God and King of the Fairies who is connected to the human dead and to the success of crops. His character in the mythology is tempestuous and mercurial, just as he appears later in folklore. Across the range of written and recorded material we find stories of Finnbheara interacting with other Gods, with fairies, and with humans. Even into the Christian period Finnbheara persisted, a being connected to a specific location but with a wider reach and reputation. Indeed, his very continuity even into the modern day is a testament to his deep imprint in human culture.

GANESH, THE REMOVER OF OBSTACLES

Janet Boyer

When my husband had to travel to Chicago for work in 2012, our son and I tagged along. At the hotel gift shop, I was delighted to see a wallet-sized picture of Ganesh, the elephant-headed god, near the cash register. "Oh, Ganapati!" I exclaimed. "I love him!" (Ganapati, as well as Ganesha, are alternative monikers for this beloved Hindu deity).

"Yes!" the Indian proprietress answered. "Would you like it?" She held it out to me. "Are you *sure*?" I stammered. Her dark eyes glittered. "Yes!"

I've kept that lovely, generous gesture in my purse ever since. Fast forward to October 2019. We took our son to the Strasburg Railroad in Lancaster, Pennsylvania for his 21st birthday—a life-long dream. We stayed at a hotel owned by Indians and, lo and behold, a huge, glorious painting of Ganesh hung behind the counter! And in my dining room, hanging on red painted walls? Why, a large, colorful tapestry—embroidered with gold sequins, no less! —depicting Ganesh surrounded by sweets and other accoutrements, a black rat near his feet. Above my desk, on the wall inside a cubicle, sits a brass state of Ganesh.

So, what's the appeal of this Hindu god, especially in commercial locales — but also in the home of a fair-skinned, aqua-eyed writer and entrepreneur? A primary reason is that Ganesh is known as the "Remover of Obstacles". In fact, devotees ask his blessing before beginning *any* undertaking, whether it be a monumental event like getting married — or something as small as planting a single seed. He's also invoked before any rite or ceremony.

A brief mantra to invoke Ganesh's blessing on new ventures is *Om Gam Ganpataye Namah*, which encourages success, prosperity and good luck. Ganpataye is yet another name for Ganesh, and this mantra translates as *"Ganesh, I bow to you — salutations to the Remover of Obstacles"*.

In addition to being the God of Beginnings, Ganesh is also the patron of arts and sciences, as well as the deva of intellect and wisdom. It's no wonder that many scribes herald him as the "Patron Saint of Writers"! (*Tip:* before starting your next writing project, be sure to invoke Ganesh — and use his mantra often to plow through creative blocks). However, I don't recommend invoking Ganesh willy-nilly or without sincerity: although he's happy to oblige helping those in the arts, he's not above *placing* obstacles in the way to garner more devotion!

Energetically, Ganesh is the embodiment of the familiar yet sacred "OM", and is said to dwell in the realm of the Muladhara (Root) Chakra.

Lord Ganesh is usually depicted with a tiny rat or mouse near his feet, because a small rodent is his steed. This diminutive creature can squeeze into all the nooks and crannies of the world and so, because the mouse is Ganesh's "vehicle", this god can do his job as the Remover of Obstacles in virtually any place, at any time.

There are several different stories as to how a chubby child, son of Shiva and Parvati (the God governing the life-force and the earth-mother) ended up with the head of an elephant—as well as to why one trunk is broken in half—but what fascinates me more, as a devotee, is the symbolism that usually surrounds depictions of Ganesh, especially since they are reminders of spiritual growth and the embodiment of wisdom.

- **Trunk:** It's been said that an elephant's trunk has the strength to uproot a tree as well as the finesse to pick up a needle. The wise person has both enormous power and fine discrimination.
- **Large Ears:** The wise listens more than talks.
- **Four Hands Holding Different Objects:** *Lotus* (symbol of enlightenment); *Hatchet* (the cutting of accumulated karma when enlightenment comes); *Laddus* (sphere-shaped sweets served during religious or festive occasions—the rewards of a life wisely lived); *Open Hand* (a blessing mudra—the wise wishes all beings well).
- **Large Stomach** – The ability to consume, and digest, all that life brings—good and bad.
- **Broken Tusk** – The wise person is beyond duality.
- **Sitting with One Foot on Knee, the Other on the Ground** –Symbolizes being "in the world, but not of it". That is, we are human and must attend to practicalities—but our source lies beyond the mundane.

Albeit familiar, this is but *one* depiction of Ganesh. For example, my wall tapestry shows him holding a rope instead of a hatchet—representing how this benevolent god pulls us closer to our ideal destiny. There are actually *thirty-two* different forms of Ganesh, each with varying symbolism—including the direction of the trunk, his posture and what he's holding (so if you're serious about obtaining or gifting images of Ganesh, you may want to do some research on which rendering best fits your needs—and honors this generous deity).

GWYDION: MASTER ENCHANTER OF BRITAIN

Elen Sentier

Gwydion gets a lot of bad press that is so undeserved and comes from lots of moral misunderstandings and prejudices, so people are unable to see him he truly is ... for he really is the Master Enchanter of Britain. His skills include:

- Master enchanter
- Master shapeshifter
- Trickster & teacher
- Maker of the body – the hallow – for Blodeuwedd, Queen of the Night
- Father of Llew Llaw Gyffes, with his sister Arianrhod
- Finder and saviour of Llew when he manages to get everything wrong and kill himself
- Bringer of the three secrets of agriculture, with his brother Amatheon, to humankind
- Winner of the Battle of the Trees with Bran so humans may keep those secrets
- Keeper of the Ash Keys
- and lots more ...

One of the most famous stories, and precursor for all that follows, is when Gwydion's brother Gilfaethwy falls in love with Goewin, Math's footholder, and Gwydion helps them make love.

When he's not at war, Math needs his footholder to keep him alive; she is a maiden who can do the magic of anchoring him to the Earth. When Math is fighting, the energies of battle enliven him, but when he's at peace he will wither and die without a maiden-footholder who can do the magic. So, Gwydion needs to get Math to fight to enable Goewin to be free to be with her lover, Gilfaethwy.

Gwydion gets an idea. He knows Pryderi, king of Dafyd, is a bit gullible and always getting things wrong, so he goes off into the forest and transforms some mushrooms into twelve beautiful stallions with golden harnesses and twelve magnificent hunting dogs. He offers the wonderful horses and dogs to Pryderi in exchange for the magical, otherworldly pigs Arawn, Lord of the Underworld, had gifted him. In his naïve greed, Pryderi jumps at the chance despite that his pact with Arawn was that he could not give the pigs to anyone else; he believes that trading them for the horses does not count as gifting. Hastily, Gwydion takes the pigs and runs for it because, at sunset, the horses and dogs will revert to being mushrooms again. As the sun goes down, Pryderi sees the beautiful stallions with all their harness, and the magical dogs, all fall apart to become mushrooms again. He's furious, feels a regular twit and calls out his army to set off for revenge. This rouses Math; he gets up, taking his feet from Goewin's lap, and sets off to war. Now Goewin and Gilfaethwy can be together.

The war is bloody so, to stop more slaughter, Pryderi meets Gwydion in single combat and Gwydion kills him. The war is now over and Math goes home ... to find he no longer has a footholder for Goewin is no longer a maid so she can no longer do the footholder-magic to anchor Math to the Earth and without her, Math will die.

Angry and afraid, Math turns his nephews into pairs of mating animals. First, Gwydion is a stag and Gilfaethwy a hind; then Gwydion is a sow and Gilfaethwy a boar; lastly Gwydion is a wolf and Gilfaethwy a she-wolf. After three years Math releases them but takes the children they bear to himself.

The Victorian story-collectors had their own cultural, moral and social agendas which colour the story so it comes over as a tale of rape and salutary punishment, not one of thwarted love. They give the impression that Goewin is happy being Math's servant, and that keeping Math alive is far more important than Goewin's happiness, or Gilfaethwy's. Gwydion is portrayed as a nasty, evil trickster, playing games for the fun of it while Pryderi is shown as a maligned monarch instead of the foolish and gullible character he shows himself to be in other stories. When you dig deep and spend time pondering the stories you come to see Gwydion as a kind helper rather than an evil trickster.

We need to learn to dig deep below the agendas and prejudices that surround us in our daily lives, we need to be awake and aware so we don't fall for all the machinations of politics, peer groups, normalcy, around us. The Master Enchanter of Britain is a good friend and brilliant teacher for this. Read his stories in as many versions as you can find, get rid of your own illusions about him brought on by the bad press the Victorian story-collectors give him. And always read with a bag of salt beside you, to dip into to keep your brain straight!

I've worked with Gwydion all my life; he's a wonderful teacher; and he's always on your side, even when he tricks you … in fact *especially* when he tricks you for then he's offering you wisdom to learn.

GWYN AP NUDD

Vanda Lloyd

Who is Gwyn? I had read about him, the legends telling how he lives under Glastonbury Tor/The Isle of Avalon. How he emerges at Samhain riding with the Wild Hunt across the land, riding with his warriors and hounds. How he re-enters his underground home each Beltane before emerging again the following Samhain. That he is also the King of the Fae, the folk who live under the hill with him, and if you entered his realm you need not eat or drink anything offered or you would not be able to leave.

Gwyn ap Nudd and Glastonbury Tor, a place I could physically explore. This was in 2016 and with a sketchy knowledge of Gwyn ap Nudd and not wanting to read any more but to walk and find what he meant to me I found myself being 'drawn' to walk on the ancient Isle of Avalon/Glastonbury Tor. I asked while I walked on the ancient hill for Gwyn to show who he was to me. I walked in all weathers, exploring once again the hill this time not to find the Goddess but Gwyn.

Walking up Glastonbury Tor via the concrete footpath and steps is easy for me if I go up from the Chalice Well side via the Fairfield but hard for me if I go up the steps from the Moneybox field side. I rarely go up Moneybox field side, I find the footpath in parts looks as if it is on a steep sideways slope and that challenges me and I become very frightened. For that reason, I always go up the other way, though longer to walk the path is easier. But as challenges go what did I find, yes, you've guessed it, I found myself quite a few times walking up the steps via the Moneybox field side, sometimes terrified but always wondering to myself 'why am I doing this?'

I found myself calling to Gwyn to help me overcome my fear, to help me get to the top of the hill. After all I didn't have the option of going back down this way, going up was bad, going down was impossible for me. So, I called to Gwyn and I would get a sense of him being there with me, helping me get past the 'very scary for me' part of the path, not looking around as I climbed but just looking at each step, I had to take to get me to the top. Why, oh why, did I do this? Then I would get to the top of the hill; breathe out a huge sigh of relief, while thanking Gwyn, and a huge sense of achievement would flow through me, I had done it. That's why I did it!

I was involved at that time in the planning for the Glastonbury Dragons Celebrations and the very first Samhain Wild Hunt. My partner, Steve had made and created the two Glastonbury

Dragons which had appeared for the very first time in May at the Beltane event. This time for Samhain he had the idea to create a throne for Gwyn ap Nudd, a throne that would carry Gwyn from the town up to the Fairfield on the lower slopes of Glastonbury Tor. The throne was built by him and I saw it emerging from those very first ideas on paper, to the first bits of wood being put together and then the actual throne completed.

A person had been chosen to be Gwyn; or I rather think Gwyn chose him than the other way around. Gwyn had not been represented in this way as a physical person at all in the town before. Despite all the myths and legends this would be the first time that he was emerging and being honored in this way. The man chosen to be Gwyn was asked to create his own mask and this he did, spending time creating, painting and putting energy into it.

The day came and Gwyn was carried on his throne to the lower slopes of Glastonbury Tor. In the growing twilight and through the man who represented him Gwyn announced his return, the first time he had done so in this way on Glastonbury Tor, the ceremony to me was a very powerful and emotional one. I then found myself standing near to Gwyn, I could see his eyes, and what I saw surprised me. I had expected him to have hard looking eyes, the eyes of a warrior, showing no emotion or feeling, but what I saw were the eyes of a warrior with kindness inside and there was warmth there. Surrounded by his tribe he looked so at home on the slopes of Glastonbury Tor. I stood for a while thinking, wondering why I was surprised that Gwyn wasn't what I had expected him to be. I realised the Gwyn I see is in the land I walk and the words that come to me and he wanted his story told of how I discovered him!

Gwyn and his Wild Hunt are now roaming the land; the King of the Fae had left his home under Glastonbury Tor and once again, for six months of the year he is wild and free.

HANUMAN

Raegan Shanti

Hanuman is the monkey headed god mentioned heavily in the Ramayana, one of the two major Sanskrit Hindu texts. He is the devoted friend to Lord Rama – an incarnation of Vishnu- and is considered a protector God.

Hanuman was born with the name Maruti, meaning "born of air" and, in some traditions, he is considered an incarnation – or Avatar- of Shiva. According to a Bhojpuri folk tale, a maiden by the name of Anjani was destined to have a special child, and Lord Rama set out to fulfil this prophecy by providing her with the seed of Shiva himself. However, it was made clear that Shiva would not be the father of the boy. When asked who Anjani's son's father would be, Lord Rama told her to wrap the baby with a shroud once he is born. The first one to lift the shroud and gaze upon his face would be his father. On the day of his birth, the shroud was lifted away from his face by the wind, and so it was decreed that Vayu, the God of Wind, was Maruti's father. His name was blessed upon him by Parvati, Saraswati and Lakshmi.

Maruti was a mischievous young child, which ultimately lead to his change in status. One day, he leapt at the sun and consumed it, believing it to be a fruit. Enraged at the loss of the sun, Indra (King of the Gods) struck him in the jaw with thunder. Vayu, his father, was furious at the mistreatment of his son and pulled away the wind from the world unless Indra bestowed powers upon Maruti. As soon as Maruti released the sun from his mouth, he was given several godlike powers, although he was cursed to be unaware of them until he needed them most. At this point, Maruti became Hanuman, referring to the strike to his jaw or *hanu*.

Hanuman met Rama during his role as the ambassador of the

Monkey King Sugriva, and immediately pledged allegiance to the prince. This set him on course to discover his powers, when Rama's wife Sita was captured by the evil King Ravana. When she refused to accept him as her new husband, Sita was thrown into a prison with the promise that she would be released if she chose to submit to him. Her location was kept secret and Rama searched for Sita for 15 years. When he found her, Hanuman was key to helping her be freed. Hanuman acted as a decoy, allowing himself to be captured by Ravana's guards, who decided to wrap his tail in rags and set it aflame. However, he had discovered his power of being able to change shape and size at will, and chose to mock the guards by growing his tail as they wrapped it, ensuring they wouldn't be able to complete this task. In frustration, they lit what they had wrapped and Hanuman sprang forth, whipping his tail all over the palace and spreading the fire. Chaos ensued, allowing Rama to break into the prison and rescue his wife. Hanuman ran ahead to the village to announce the good news, and the villagers lit the forest with small oil lamps so the reunited couple could be guided home.

Over millennia, Hanuman served as a dedicated friend to Rama and his family. Most notably, during a great battle, Hanuman was sent to gather healing herbs to treat the wounded, which included Laksman, Rama's brother. When it was clear that picking the herbs would cost time they didn't have, Hanuman uprooted the entire mountain and brought it back to the ailing.

From these stories, it is clear how Hanuman cemented his role as that of the Protector. Whilst he is mainly seen as Lord Rama's companion, in many sects of Hinduism he is a full god in his own right. He is associated with wit and cunning, as well as male strength and virility. As time progressed, he also became associated with female fertility as well. Hanuman is also the patron god of wrestlers.

His sacred days are Saturday and Tuesday (depending on

the sect). On the chosen sacred day, his followers provide offerings to his image, and his statues are annointed. Basil, saffron and jasmine flowers are sacred to him, and he is also fond of guava and the Indian sweet *ladoo*. Statues of Hanuman are often red and/or annointed with jasmine oil and saffron, which can also be used on the worshipper to gain confidence. To worship Hanuman is to seek protection against evil spirits and evil humans, aid concentration and wit and to gain power over one's enemies.

HAR PAR KRAT

Connie Pina Rounds

Every soul carries secrets waiting to be awakened. The soul leads you down a path of initiation and reveals what you are made of on the inside. *"To know, to dare, to will and to keep silent,"* these are the four pillars of what most Pagans refer to as The Witches Pyramid and what Ceremonial Magicians refer to as the Four Powers of the Magus. These principals are the steps that an initiate of magic walks to awaken those mysteries.

My first experience with magic was around 13 years ago. I purchased a tarot spell book at the bookstore and a small flyer floated out of the book as I flipped through the pages. It was for a local Golden Dawn group. I was already very green to Witchcraft and Paganism, but Golden Dawn was a subject completely unknown to me. At the time there was really not a whole lot of information about Golden Dawn on the internet. The little flyer listed some of the things they studied and tarot was included.

So, after a month of mustering up my courage, I called them up and drove to their temple to meet them in person. It was located in a pretty run down desolate area in the Chicago, IL area, but when you stepped through the door the most beautiful

Golden Dawn temple existed. I joined the group during the Autumnal Equinox. People had traveled from other states and countries to be part of this celebration at the time. Initiations and classes were happening all weekend long.

It is in the Golden Dawn Neophyte Initiation that I took my first step *"to know, to dare, to will and most especially to keep silent."* And it is this initiation that I heard the name Har Par Krat uttered for the first time, when the grand word of the Neophyte grade was being given.

Har Par Krat is the Egyptian God of Silence. He is referred to as, Horus the Child, often presented as a young boy sitting or standing on top of a Lotus flower. The tip of his index finger rests upon his lips. In the Golden Dawn initiation, Har Par Krat, is used as reminder to keep your oath of secrecy. Although, today much of their knowledge is already mainstream thanks to members such as Israel Regardie and Aleister Crowley. Still, members are currently asked to take that oath for reasons such as, not to share who the other members are with the public and not to share the extensive knowledge you gain through the given material and members teaching the group.

Why is secrecy such an important part of magic? I can tell you that when I joined this magical secret society, I told no one for the first several months. I didn't want to ask for anyone else's opinion. I didn't want to be swayed by anyone else's ideas. There was no negative thoughts coming my way. And no person to say, "I wish you wouldn't be part of that group."

Having the attitude of Har Par Krat allowed for me to be a child learning the magic of the spirits and the elements around me with no distractions. It allowed me to be brave and try new things like invoking and astral projection. It allowed me to experience the wonder of my own will without the worries of outside influences. I used magic to get promoted at work with a $20,000 raise and got to learn a whole new set of skills that would make me a more desirable employee. Har Par Krat taught me the importance of silence.

As far as easy and practical everyday magic goes, I like to use Har Par Krat as a cloak of silence. I work in technology and handle application and network outages. Some days it gets busy and I don't mind. But when things start to feel out of control busy, I call on Har Par Krat. I vibrate his name and feel his energy come down from the universe and wrap around me like a mummy. Once I feel fully cloaked by that energy, I make the sign of silence. My left index finger touches my lips. And most often times, a sense of calmness in the storm will come through shortly after that. If the entire room is in chaos, I will vibrate silently and allow the energy to fill the entire room before I give the sign of silence.

Some days, if I feel like I want a quiet day with no worries, I start my day with the vibration of Har Par Krat first thing in the morning. And at the end of that much needed cloak of silence, I like to say a little Thanks for the help to Har Par Krat, as I imagine that energy dissipating back to the universe. This can easily be used for other similar situations. If you prefer to blend into the background at a social gathering of some sort. If you are speeding past a cop, quickly vibrate Har Par Krat with your fingers crossed.

There are several ways to meditate, but sometimes it is just nice to sit in the silence. It gives you time to acknowledge your thoughts and let them go. Ask Har Par Krat to help you let go of the heaviness of your day and find the child that exists inside you while you sit quietly.

Regardless, of what magical path you are on, Har Par Krat, is a wonderful god to call upon for any acts of secrecy. He will remind you that you are a keeper of spiritual knowledge and to proceed with caution. He will remind you to approach your magic with a heart that is child-like and pure. Don't be afraid to let Har Par Krat make you laugh in a moment of silence. I cannot imagine getting through some of my more chaotic moments without him.

HEPHAESTUS

Kenn Payne

As with most of the Greek Pantheon, drop a name to someone and they'll usually come back at you with a rather abridged explanation of what that God or Goddess represents. Hephaestus for example, would often be referred to as the "smith god" or "the ugly craftsman with a limp". And as with all the Greek Pantheon, Hephaestus is so much more than that. As the God of blacksmiths, metalworking, carpenters, craftsmen, artisans, sculptors, metallurgy, fire, and volcanoes He is a potent and driven creative force.

His divine parentage is either that He is the son of Zeus and Hera or that he was born of Hera alone; the latter myth sometimes being interpreted that Hera's attempt to create offspring without the aid of Her husband (like Zeus managed with the birth of Athena) is what lead to the deformity and disability that was instantly noticeable.

Many myths allude to how He became an initial outcast and injured. The main line says that He was cast off Mount Olympus by Hera because of he was *"shrivelled of foot"*. Another account puts it down to Zeus, who throws Him down from Olympus for protecting Hera from Zeus's advances.

After His fall, Hephaestus was raised beneath the ocean waves by the Goddess Thetis (mother of famed Achilles) and the Oceanid Eurynome. During His time beneath the waves, He never quite got over the way He was treated by Hera and so gifted at crafts and invention was He, that he devised a plan to take his revenge.

He made Hera a beautiful and magical golden throne that Hephaestus sent to Her as a peace offering, but when Hera sat on it, She found that She could no longer stand up! After numerous fruitless attempts by the other Olympians to free

Her, Hera frantically and emotionally pleaded that someone fetch Hephaestus. But unfortunately, despite the pleas of both the other Gods and His mother, Hephaestus refused.

And so, it was another outsider from Olympus that offered salvation. Dionysos, the God of wine, ecstasy and madness agreed to visit Hephaestus and talk Him round. And at last, intoxicated with wine and slumped on the back of a donkey, Hephaestus was returned and after a little more coercion, He finally agreed to release Hera, who though embarrassed, outraged and shamed, forgave Him and asked for forgiveness Herself, for how She had treated Him.

And of course, it was not the last time that the wily Hephaestus would utilise his divine skills of crafting and creation. Not only did He forge many gifts and weapons for His fellow Olympians, but he also sought revenge after he discovered that his wife, the goddess of love Aphrodite, had been having an affair with Ares, god of war. He devised a plan by crafting a fine, gilded net so sheer that it was almost invisible and yet despite its gossamer form it was as strong as adamantine.

And so, when next Aphrodite and Ares took to bed together, the net fell over them and trapped them in the act, whereupon Hephaestus brought all the other Olympians to view the spectacle, thoroughly humiliating his wife and her infuriated lover.

As an Olympian his myths and cult were quite broad and he was involved in many tales such as the crafting of the first woman, Pandora, at the command of Zeus. His attempt to take the sworn virgin Athena as a lover which when rebuffed resulted in the impregnation of Earth and the birth of Erikhthonios, one of the early kings of Athens. His skilled craftmanship was responsible for the creation of a cursed necklace that belonged to Harmonia, which doomed her descendants to a cycle of tragedy. During the Trojan War Hephaestus fought the river-god Skamandros with fire. And the crafting of Achille's armour at the request of His adoptive mother, Thetis.

In a modern sense, Hephaestus is a skilled craftsman and overcomer of obstacles, having played to his strengths despite abandonment, rejection, ridicule and disability. As the God of Crafts and the Forge, He reflects the powerful creative forces found within each of us. He is pragmatic and does what needs to be done, valuing hard work, honesty, dependability and loyalty.

Ways in which you can tap into His powers and honour Him include taking up a craft or skill such as metalwork or anything else where you need to work with your hands. Support local and independent craftspeople – value their time and energy. Working alongside those with disabilities and supporting their rights. You could also work to promote peace and reconciliation. He encourages us to tackle our problems swiftly and with decisiveness, working around obstacles and limitations to create a positive outcome. And He's not adverse to a little tipple of wine or beer should you wish to earn extra blessings.

HERMES

Samantha leaver

Who is the Greek God you see the most influence in your everyday life? Hermes. Known to the Romans as Mercury, he is the ancient Greek God of roads, journeys, merchants, athletes, thieves, trickery, animal husbandry, and a handful of other related things and the thing is, he's very good at all of it.

He is predominately recognised as a messenger god but was also revered as an underworld god and a psychopomp responsible for guiding the souls of the dead, including bringing Persephone back from Hades to cheer up her mother and reignite Earth's growth.

Along with Hekate, Hermes is the only God given the power

to move between, the below (Hades), Earth, and the above (Olympus). For this reason, some Hellenic Pagans may work with Hermes to increase their ability to speak with spirits, have visitations and even in funerary rites to guide their loved ones to the afterlife. He also pulls a triple shift guiding dreams and has a hobby on the side of helping mortal heroes.

Hermes is very young by Olympian standards, only Dionysos is chronologically younger. He is born to the Pleiade Maia in the mountains in Arcadia and is unsurprisingly the son of Zeus. Hermes sets himself apart from other Olympians by getting his trickery underway the day he is born. According to the Homeric Hymn to Hermes, the first thing he does is find a tortoise, kill it and use its entrails and shell to make a Lyre. Then he steals 50 of his brother Apollon's sacred cattle. But in case Apollon notices his sacred cows are missing, Hermes reverses their hooves, so it looks like they're walking backwards. Hermes hides the cattle and starts a fire so he can sacrifice the meat to the Gods and himself, and then returns home. His mum isn't buying the innocent baby look, so Hermes explains to her that this is all part of his cunning plan to put himself on the Olympians radar so he can get them both the respect and honour they deserve, instead of living in a cave.

Meanwhile Apollon has noticed his cows are missing and after a little detective work, he tracks down Hermes in Maia's cave. Apollon interrogates Hermes and brings him to Zeus, who thinks this entire situation is hilarious and tells Hermes to guide Apollon to the cows. On the way, Hermes wins Apollon over by playing the Lyre. Apollon is so enchanted that he promises Hermes will be the messenger of the Gods and he and his mother will be honoured among the Olympians.

As messenger of the Gods, he is known to be swift footed and he got his winged sandals from Hephaestus not long after this. Along with Apollon in his oracular aspect, many Hellenic Pagans honour Hermes, asking him to deliver messages to us mortals through divination (sacred to Apollon), dreams, and or physical signs, be they in nature or as technology has advanced through media like TV, books and social media. He is also the god of commerce. Back to the myth – Apollon agrees to exchange the lyre for the cattle and promising Hermes will never rob him again Apollon gives him his Caduceus, a small staff with snakes coiled around it, usually seen as a symbol of messengers and heralds, an astrologically ancient symbol of commerce and thought to represent Hermes ability to fly (not to be confused with Asklepios' rod which symbolises healing and medicine)

Hermes makes his debut as a trickster underdog, achieving an improbable victory through cunning and trickery and despite winning untold power and fame in the process somehow still manages to remain as the trickster underdog for centuries to come.

Hermes makes regular appearances in mythology, playing a supporting role in both the Iliad and the Odyssey. In the Iliad, although he was allied with the Achaenans, he also protected King Priam when he travelled to the Achaenan camp to retrieve the body of his son Hector, and in the Odyssey, Hermes provided regular help and advice to Odysseus, including helping him confront Circe to break her enchantment on his men and later guiding the dead souls of the suitors to the afterlife. This extra amount of assistance might have been because Odysseus is his great grandson.

One of Hermes most well-known accomplishments is killing the hundred eyed giant Argos, in the myth of Io. For somewhat complicated reasons the nymph Io ends up getting turned into a white heifer and kept under the watchful guard of Argos, Zeus asks Hermes to free her, so Hermes disguises himself as a simple shepherd, lures Argos to sleep with a long and boring story about the creation of the panpipes, then cuts off his head. To commemorate the occasion Hermes is referred to with the epithet Argeiphontes meaning "Slayer of Argos".

Hermes has a handful of appearances in other popular Greek Mythology, he helps errant heroes like Perseus by giving him the means to sneak around invisibly, for example, by borrowing Hades Helm of Invisibility. In fact, trickery is the major characteristic of Hermes.

Hermes is the God of liars and thieves, and although this might not seem the most positive of qualities for a god to instil, most heroes were tricksters or underdogs on some level.

HERNE THE HUNTER

Arietta Bryant

The very first God-Images which I felt a connection towards, were those featuring a tall, rugged, masculine figure, usually bare chested and always adorned with antlers – although whether these are his horns or whether they are part of some form of ritual clothing is variable according to different depictions. I came to know this deity as Herne the Hunter, Horned God of the Hunt.

The more I looked for information about Herne, a deity I had mainly come to know on an intuitive level, the more I found his legend tangled and overlapped with other similar horned figures. Herne is just one of many characters from myth, legend, history and folktale, who have been used to represent an aspect of the Horned God within Wicca and Paganism.

Perhaps some of my natural connection to Herne is geographical. Herne's legend hails from the English county of Berkshire which is the next county along from where I have lived for most of my life. In the Berkshire City of Windsor, he is famed to this day as the spectral hunter who may be found wandering in Windsor Great Park. Historically, the tree known as Herne's Oak was said to be his favourite spot, sadly this no longer exists, perhaps destroyed by lightning; although there are some who believe it was cut down by King George III.

One of the earliest written accounts of the Herne story comes to us through William Shakespeare and his play, 'The Merry Wives of Windsor':

> "There is an old tale goes, that Herne the hunter, sometime a keeper here in Windsor Forest, doth all the winter-time, at still midnight, walk round about an oak, with great ragged horns; and there he blasts the tree and takes the cattle and makes milch-kine yield blood and shakes a chain in a most hideous and dreadful manner."

Even this early written account refers to the tale as "old", suggesting that Shakespeare did not create this tale, it is drawn from older folk tales and therefore it has already been around for a long while. I imagine that many of those in the audience in 1597 would have some awareness of Herne The Hunter.

Herne is interesting to research in that there is some evidence to suggest he was a real man; however, most facts have been lost to time and we only have stories and hearsay to go on. One pervasive and popular legend suggests that Herne was caught poaching in Windsor Great Forest. Unable to live with this shame he hung himself from an old oak tree.

Herne is worshiped as an aspect of the Horned God within Paganism, and he is often seen as similar to the Gaulish deity, Cernunnos. Cernunnos is a Celtic Deity also linked to hunting and I have seen it suggested that Herne is somehow a variant of Cerne – meaning 'Horn' in Latin perhaps meaning that they could be the same person.

Throughout the history and folklore of Europe, there are many variations on the wild huntsman myth. Many of these tell of a ghostly warrior leading a moonlit hunt. a Celtic forest guardian left to haunt a great oak. In Anglo-Saxon belief Herne was seen as more of a Deity than a ghost, but later, as Christianity gained popularity the tales of the hunt became more fearsome and violent, cementing the connection between this life and the next.

It seems that across many different cultures, in each settlement, there will have been a named hunter who was given praise and even worshiped as a deity. Whilst not all of these will have been Herne there will have been similarities and as settlements grew and knowledge was shared many of these Hunter Gods will have become homogenised into the few whom we still recall today.

To build a connection to Herne I would recommend taking yourself off and finding a wooded area to sit in. feel the ground beneath you and lean against a tree, imagine all the history which has passed by this spot. Use all of your senses, perhaps the tree behind you is no longer a tree, perhaps now you are leaning against the legs of a tall strong man as he waits, in readiness, for the hunt.

HYPNOS

Kenn Payne

After breathing, eating, reproducing and dying one of the oldest habits of humankind is probably sleeping and so it is of no great consequence that such a mysterious act – where the body seems almost to "die" in the physical world – would be personified as a divine being.

To the Greeks, this was Hypnos, a winged young man who dwelt in the land of eternal darkness beyond the gates of the rising sun, known as Erebos. Each night, he would rise into the sky following in the train of his mother, the Goddess Nyx (night). He was often seen alongside his twin brother, Thanatos (Peaceful Death), and it was said that the Oneiroi (Dreams) were either his brothers or sons.

Symbols attributed to Him include many sleep-related items and He was often depicted carrying either a horn of sleep-inducing opium, a poppy-stem, a branch dripping water from the river Lethe (Forgetfulness), or an inverted torch. His cult was sometimes linked to that of the healer god, Asclepius and this was probably due to the connection with sleep, healing and dream incubation where the healing god was believed to visit supplicants of the shrine in their dreams.

The mystery of sleep must have been both thought-provoking and terrifying for earlier civilizations, and the tales of those who returned with recollection of dreams must have fascinated the curious mind.

Even today, sleep and dreams can be both beneficial and revelatory. Working closely and with respect to the personification of Sleep and to one of the keepers of dream spirits can not only help you find a balance of mind, body and spirit through rest and recuperation but also tap in to the deep and diverse messages that come from the Dream Spirits.

We can consciously ask Hypnos to deliver deep and restful sleep (much needed in this hectic and fast-paced world) as well as petition Him to send pleasant and informative dreams. A whole mini-ritual can be built around the act of going to sleep, with mindful intent. We don't have to burn the midnight oil until we pass out in a chair or fall half-dressed into our beds. Sleeping is a purposeful and divine gift and by honouring it and Hypnos, we can develop a better right relationship with the nature of sleep and the dream spirits.

There are many dream-interpretation books and websites out there, but the fundamental principle of dreams and their symbolism is an inherently personal one. What does what you see and experience in the dream state truly mean to you? This might take some practice and perseverance to become objective enough to see all the possible angles but once we start receiving clearer messages that can be acted on and utilized to create positive change in our lives, we can thank Hypnos and His dream spirit entourage.

INARI

Mélusine Draco

Inari is one of the most popular of Japanese gods and possibly the most complex, with more than one-third of the Shinto shrines being dedicated to him. Son of the impetuous storm god, Tsusanoo, he is the protector of rice cultivation; furthering prosperity and worshiped by merchants and tradesmen, he is also the patron deity of sword-smiths and associated with brothels and entertainers – as well as being an all-round general problem solver. Represented as male or female, he is identified with *Uka no Mitama no Kami* ('August Spirit of Food') and with the goddess of food, *Ukemochi no Kami.* Usually when referring to Inari, the two general images are of an old man sitting on a pile of rice with two foxes beside him, or of a beautiful fox-woman.

Inari became the patron of blacksmiths and the protector of warriors as his worship spread across Japan during the Edo period. Inari helped the swordsmith Sanjō Munechika forge the blade *kokitsune-maru* (Little Fox) in the late 10th century – the subject of the Noh drama *Sanjo Kokaji.* while a woodblock print from the Gekkō Zuihitsu series depicts Munechika forging the *kokitsune* for the Emperor Ichijō, with Inari and a troop of ethereal foxes lending their aid. Inari often appeared to warriors and for this reason became the yashikigami, or household deity of the samurai.

There are several theories on how foxes became Inari's servants. The first tells of a family of foxes who travelled to the shrine at Inari Mountain to offer their service to Inari, who granted their request and placed them as the attendants of the shrine. Another comes from the behavior of living foxes often seen in and around rice fields during the growing season eating the rodents that would otherwise consume the rice; giving them an image of guardians of the fields. Also significant is the colour of the fur resembles that of ripened rice, and its tail looks like a full sheaf of rice.

Primarily, however, Inari is associated with agriculture, protecting rice fields and giving the farmers an abundant harvest every year. One myth celebrated in popular folk festivals tells of him coming down the mountain every spring for planting season and ascending back up the mountain after the harvest for the winter. The entrance to an Inari shrine is marked by one or more vermilion *torii* and statues of *kitsune*, which are often adorned with red *yodarekake* (votive bibs). This red colour has come to be identified with Inari, because of its use at his shrines. Fushimi Inari Taisha temple complex is the oldest, largest and most important: the paths having over 5,000 torii, placed so close together as to form covered walkways.

Fox sculptures at his shrines wear their red bibs for good luck and hold a key to a rice granary in their mouths. Each shrine also has a symbolic hole in one of its perimeter walls to allow Inari's fox messengers ease of entry and exit. Worshippers leave offers for the fox, typically inari-zushi, which is cooked rice wrapped in fried tofu and soaked in a sweet rice liquor, in the hope that the fox will pass on good things about the worshipper and ensure a favourable response from the god.

Inari in female form, however, is a creature to be handled with care. A common belief in medieval Japan was that any woman encountered alone, especially at dusk or after dark, could be a fox. A *kitsune's* shape-shifting abilities are not limited by the fox's age or gender, and it can duplicate the appearance of a specific person although they are particularly renowned for impersonating beautiful women whose tell-tale signs are a fox-shaped shadow, or a reflection that shows its true form.

Inari is one of the more mysterious *kami* and a priest at the

Fushimi shrine commented on this diversity said: '*If there were one hundred worshippers, they will have one hundred different ideas about Inari.*' And trying to categorize him as merely the Old Man of Rice or in the female aspect of Dakiniten, would be to overlook the diversity that is imbedded in Shinto belief. In order to study Inari, we have to look beyond any one representation in order to have a well-rounded view of this enigmatic *kami*.

Inari remains a popular figure in both Shinto and Buddhist beliefs in Japan and modern corporations often revere him as a patron with shrines at their corporate headquarters. Inari's traditional festival day is the sixth day of the second month (*nigatsu no hatsuuma*) of the luni-solar calendar. In some parts of Kyūshū, a festival begins five days before the full moon in November; occasionally it is extended to a full week and is accompanied by bringing offerings of rice products to a shrine to Inari each day and receiving *o-mamori* (protection charms) in return.

KWANNON – GODDESS OF MERCY, LORD OF COMPASSION

Mélusine Draco

One of the most common deities encountered around Japan will be a slender androgynous figure, known popularly as Kannon-Kwannon-sama. The proper Japanese name is Kanzeon Bosatsu. Kwannon personifies compassion and is one of the most widely worshipped divinities in Asia in both ancient and modern times, being a *Bosatsu* – one who achieves enlightenment but postpones *nirvana* until all can be saved.

Originally depicted with masculine features, Kwannon later appears with attributes of both genders, eventually becomes a symbol of the 'divine feminine' in many East Asian countries; with each culture showing Kwannon in different forms to suit their own temperaments and spiritual concepts. Kwannon is considered male in the Buddhist traditions of India, Tibet, and Southeast Asia but in China and less so in Japan, around c.11th century Kwannon was commonly portrayed as female.

Kwannon's femininity is clearly compatible with Japanese religious sensibilities because unlike Buddhism, whose deities are generally genderless or male, Japan's Shintō tradition has long revered the female element. The emperor of Japan, even today, claims direct decent from Amaterasu (the supreme Shintō Sun Goddess), so it's only natural that Kwannon was given feminine attributes. According to Japanese scholar, John Nelson:

"Kwannon has been so widely dispersed in Japanese culture, like the air one breathes, she has become part of the social and cultural landscape in ways that transcend sectarian doctrine ... Perhaps we are limiting the possibilities by thinking of Kwannon as a specifically Buddhist deity. Surely it makes as much sense in the context of the Japanese religious culture to see her role as similar to that of a Shintō kami – specific to the situations of any place and its people, and attentive to sincere petitions."

Kwannon's identification with the needs of women emerged in the Heian period (9-12th centuries) with effigies associated with the virtues of compassion, gentleness, purity of heart, and motherhood appearing in female form. In early Japanese-Buddhism the concept of venerating a female statue would have been unthinkable but later statues clearly portray the deity as female. The classical sculptors of Buddhist imagery carved the faces, bodies, and robes in ways that transcended male and female forms. Nonetheless, the orthodox view remained that all Buddha and Bodhisattva were male and one indication is that many archaic statues in Japan sport mustaches: a closer look will often reveal that the 'goddess' has a mustache!

Kwannon's worship remains non-denominational and widespread, appearing in countless forms throughout Japan to assist with all manner of earthly petitions and he is the guardian of those born in the Year of the Rat. As Batō Kwannon, he is depicted as horse-headed and becomes the protector of animals, particularly those who labour for mankind; extending those powers to protecting their spirits and bringing them ease and a happier life than they experienced while on earth. Many archaic stone statues (*sekibutsu*) of Batō were once set in place to protect travelers and their horses from injury on dangerous paths; he also became associated with a Shintō *kami* who rides between this world and the sacred realm, and patron of the *Komagata*, or horse-shaped shrines found all over Japan.

Also known as Dōbutsu Kannon – a modern form devoted to the care of suffering animals. This modern-day interpretation as a patron of dead pets is not surprising since there are numerous antecedents. Batō Kwannon, for example, as an esoteric saviour of those reborn in the realm of animals was already well-known among the common folk in the Tokugawa period, when farmers prayed to him for the safety and preservation of their livestock, and innumerable stone steles of Batō Kwannon were erected during the Tokugawa and Edo periods. Japanese scholar Mark R. Mullins in his article 'The Many Forms and Functions of Kannon in Japanese Religion and Culture' writes: *"Kannon has become a favorite comforting figure used by the numerous pet cemeteries that have been built across Japan over the past two decades."*

Gigantic effigies of Kwannon are known as Dai-Kannon and Japan has always had a penchant for constructing massive statues; many erected post-WWII with a view to increasing tourism to certain Japanese localities, while others were erected to pray for world peace and the repose of the war dead. The Ryōzen Kwannon of Kyoto was made with 500 tons of concrete to commemorate the soldiers who died in WWII and to pray for a peaceful Japan.

Another contemporary role for Kwannon, according to Mark Mullins, is connected to the ageing Japanese society and the increasing concerns of the elderly about growing old, fears of senile dementia and long illnesses followed by an unpleasant death. Kwannon's powers have been expanded to include the 'suppression of senility' and has become a central figure in temples where the elderly go to pray for a sudden or painless death. Kwannon – Goddess of Mercy, Lord of Compassion therefore gives a universal appeal to this androgynous deity's attributes since they are those of a colossus that straddles the world.

LUGH

Tiffany Lazic

One of the great champions of Ireland (as is his son, Cú Chulainn), Lugh is a multi-faceted god through whom many key family threads come together. The son of Cian (of the Tuatha De Danann) and Ethniu (of the Fomorians). On his father's side, his grandfather is the great physician, Dian Cecht; his uncle is Miach, the master surgeon; and his aunt is Airmid, the tragic herbalist. On his mother's side, he is the grandson of the Fomorian king, Balor whose terrible poisonous evil eye was said to decimate whomever it gazed upon. The tale of Lugh's birth is a version of the "thwarted birth gone awry" myth. When Balor is confronted with the prophesy that he will be killed by his own grandson, he looks to change this destiny by locking his daughter, Ethniu in a tower (Tór Mór) to ensure she has no contact with men. As these attempts rarely unfold as anticipated, Balor's desire to possess a very special cow results in a chain of events that ultimately leads to Ethniu bearing Cian triplets. Balor intends to have all three babes drowned but the messenger charged with this task accidentally drops one child on the way to the river and thus, Lugh survives the first treacherous obstacles of his life. The *Lebor Gabála Érenn* says his father, Cian then gives him to Tailtiu (of the Fir Bolg) to be fostered, creating a link between Lugh and three of the major ancient tribes of Ireland (Tuatha De Danann, Fomorians, and Fir Bolg). Another version of the tale says that he actually was tossed in the sea, but rescued by Manannán mac Lir who delivered him to Tailtiu. Lugh's fondness for his foster-mother was great, as is evident by his establishment of the Tailteann Games held in her honour during Lughnasadh (August 1). Otherwise known as the Assembly of Lugh, this time marked the beginning of the harvest and the triumph of effort over blight in the anticipated abundant crop.

Known by many names including Lugh Lámfada (Lugh of the Long Arm) and Lugh Samildánach (Equally Skilled in Many Arts), he encompasses a divine energy that is hard to pin down. Due to his connection with the late Summer festival of Lughnasadh, there can be a tendency to see Lugh as a solar deity, but it is perhaps more accurate to see him as a deity of mastery, rather than Light. Not only skilled in the warrior arts, Lugh is said to be a master builder and craftsman, a smith, a poet, a harpist, and even, with Manannán mac Lir as his foster-father, a sorcerer. It is through his wide range of skills that he gains entrance to the court of the king of the Tuatha De Danann, Nuada, whose own tale is central to the heart-breaking situation that unfolded between Lugh's paternal relatives, Dian Cecht, Miach, and Airmid. Stopped by the court doorkeeper who demands Lugh offer a skill of worth in service to the king before being able to cross the threshold, Lugh provides a litany of his considerable skills and abilities. However, after each one, the doorkeeper replies that the king already has someone at court to fulfil that task. On and on goes this exchange until finally Lugh counters with a question of his own: "Does the king have someone who holds all these skills simultaneously?" In fact, the king does not and Lugh is granted entrance to the court where he quickly proves his worth to such a degree that, when the Tuatha De Danann decide to rise up against their oppressors, The Fomorians, he is put in charge of the army. In this, the

Second Battle of Mag Tuired, Lugh finds himself on the battle field against his maternal grandfather, Balor.

Along with his unquestionable skill, Lugh has the benefit of several magical items invaluable to a warrior: the Spear of Assail, said to be irrepressible in its thirst for battle and unfailing in its ability to hit its mark when a certain incantation is said over it; Fragarach, the sword of Manannán mac Lir, which speaks to the fondness between Lugh and his foster-father; and a mighty sling-stone, which Lugh uses to kill Balor, driving his sling-stone so powerfully into Balor's eye that the eyeball is propelled towards the Fomorian army wreaking terrible havoc on the opposing forces. As Nuada has been tragically killed in the Second Battle of Mag Tuired, Lugh becomes king of the Tuatha De Danaan, freeing them from oppression and securing valuable information about solid and beneficial agricultural practices form the Fomorians.

These wondrous tales just scratch the surface of this complex god. As is expected of a champion, he is involved in a multitude of events, altercations, and adventures throughout his kingship. He inspires us to step courageously into challenging situations; to be open to learn from many masters in order to see our own multidimensionality; and to take the time to honour those individuals who have aided and supported us along the way. He invites us to look oppression in the eye and when it is forced to back down, he brings merciful negotiation to the table in a way that is beneficial to all. In these ways, he serves as a shining example to encourage the best within ourselves.

MABON

Jhenah Telyndru

Mabon is the Divine Youth of Welsh tradition. It is believed that his tale originated in Pagan Celtic times and existed in oral tradition for centuries before being committed to writing in the medieval period; because of this, like all figures in Welsh lore, he is not directly identified as a divinity in his stories. However, there are many clues which point to his divine nature, including the meaning of his full name, Mabon ap Modron, which translates as "Divine Youth, son of the Divine Mother."

In the 11th century tale *Culhwch ac Olwen*, we learn that the infant Mabon was stolen from his mother Modron when he was only three nights old; no one knew if he were alive or dead, and if alive, where he had been hidden. Several warriors from King Arthur's court take up the cause to find Mabon as part of a larger quest they have embarked upon. They seek the council of the Oldest Animals of the Island of the Mighty – the Blackbird of Cilgwri, the Stag of Redynvre, the Owl of Cwm Cawlwyd, and the Eagle of Gwern Abwy — hoping they would know Mabon's whereabouts, but each, more ancient than the last, had not heard of him.

Finally, the Salmon of Llyn Llyw, the fifth and oldest animal of all, leads Arthur's men to the place of Mabon's imprisonment in Caer Loyw (Gloucester), where they hear him cry out:

"...he who is here has reason to lament. It is Mabon son of Modron who is imprisoned here, and no one has been so painfully incarcerated in a prison as I, neither the prison of Lludd Llaw Eraint, nor the prison of Graid son of Eri." (Davies, 2007, pg. 205)

The warriors lay siege to the fort and set the prisoner free. Mabon is then able to participate in the hunt of the enchanted wild boar Twrch Trwyth. Riding a horse as swift as a wave, beside a dog who obeys only him, he is able to obtain the razor hidden between the boar's ears, one of the *anetheau*, or difficult things, necessary – like his own liberation – to successfully complete the quest.

Mabon's imprisonment is further attested in *Trioedd Ynys Prydein* (*The Triads of the Island of Britain*):

Triad 52: Three Exalted Prisoners of the Island of Britain:

Llyr Half-Speech, who was imprisoned by Euroswydd,
and the second, Mabon son of Modron,
and third, Gwair son of Geirioedd. (Bromwich, 2006, p. 146)

Mabon's association with the motif of the Exalted Prisoner is an important aspect of his character. In later Arthurian tales, we find storylines associated with imprisonment which feature characters whose names – Mabonagrain, Maboun, and Mabuz – are cognates, or derivatives, of the Welsh name Mabon. Further, scholars believe that *Y Mabinogi* – the collective title for the Four Branches, which are four interrelated tales from early Welsh literature – translates to "Tales of the Youth", and that it is so named because they refer to a cycle of stories concerning Mabon ap Modron.

While Mabon is never mentioned in *Y Mabinogi*, there is only one character who appears in all Four Branches: Pryderi, son of Rhiannon. This is significant because Pryderi, like Mabon, was stolen from his mother as a newborn and later becomes imprisoned in an Otherworldly fortress; both characters are hunters shown in pursuit of an Otherworldly boar, and both have affinities for dogs and horses. It is possible, therefore, that Pryderi is a reflex of Mabon – a mythological inheritor of his tales.

This is important because Mabon himself is a reflex of the Continental Celtic deity Maponos ("Divine Youth") who is the son of Matrona ("Divine Mother"), known in Wales as Modron. The Mother-Son Dyad was an important aspect of his cultus, and he was often worshiped together with Matrona, who was the Goddess of the river Marne in France and was herself believed to be a singular form of the triple Matronae worshiped widely on the European Continent.

The Romans saw this Gallic god as a resonance of Apollo, and based on ancient inscriptions and altar dedications, we see that they came to worship him in the syncretized form of Apollo Maponos. It appears that the cultus of Maponos spread from the continent, coming eventually to thrive in Britain, especially in and around Hadrian's Wall, where we have abundant archaeological evidence of his worship. Although the myths of Maponos have been lost to us, the general core of his story may have been preserved in the characters from British and Arthurian lore who appear to be his mythic reflexes.

In modern Neo-Pagan tradition, the name "Mabon" was assigned to the Autumn Equinox by author Aidan Kelly in 1974; he writes that he did so because he was unaware of any Pagan names for the equinox. Noting that the Eleusinian Mysteries of Demeter and Kore began on the full moon nearest the fall equinox, and seeking a similar take from Celtic tradition, he found that the story of Mabon's imprisonment most closely reminded him of the journey of Kore – whose name means "Maiden", just as Mabon's means "Youth" – into the Underworld and back. Today, Pagans who use the name Mabon for the Autumn Equinox have found meaningful symbolism in its association with the Welsh divinity, but it is important to note that there is no ancient, cultural, or mythological association between the God and the holy day.

MANAWYDAN FAB LLŶR

Kris Hughes

Manawydan fab Llŷr is well known to students of the Mabinogi, but to most people He is just a deity whose name is strikingly similar to the Irish Manannán mac Lir. Their names are too alike for there not to be a connection, but their myths are very different.

Manawydan/Manannán means "one from the Isle of Man" (a large island in the Irish Sea) but it is not clear whether the island takes its name from the deity, or vice versa. *Fab Llŷr* simply means "son of Llŷr". Llŷr means "sea" or "ocean" and is also the name of a shadowy ancestor-deity. There were Irish settlements in southern Wales, where Manawydan's main myth takes place, in the 2nd century AD, and the Isle of Man, itself, has felt influences from Irish, Scottish, Welsh, English and Norse culture over the centuries, which helps us understand the connection.

We first meet Manawydan in the Second Branch of the Mabinogi, as the brother of the high king, Bran, and their sister, Branwen. Their mother is Penarddun, daughter of another ancestor-god, Beli Mawr. Manawydan accompanies Bran on his adventures in Ireland, but His part in the action is not singled out.

In the Third Branch, Manawydan is central to the story and we finally get to know Him. After a devastating battle in the Second Branch, Manawydan is invited to the southern kingdom of Dyfed by Pryderi, the son of the famous horse-sovereignty goddess, Rhiannon. Pryderi offers Manawydan the kingdom of Dyfed and the widowed Rhiannon's hand in marriage. He agrees, and Pryderi, his wife Cigfa, and the newlyweds, quickly become fast friends.

Soon, a mysterious mist falls on Dyfed, which causes all the people, farms, and cattle to disappear. Manawydan begins to show himself to be a wise counsellor, or father figure, doing his best to control the hot-headed Pryderi's impulses, and to sooth the anxious Cigfa.

After a period of living off the land, Manawydan suggests that they go to England and take up a trade. However, the four are too skilled at each trade they try and are always driven away by the local tradesmen. Each time Manawydan must talk Pryderi out of fighting the locals.

Eventually, they go back to Dyfed and one day, Pryderi and Manawydan chase a white boar which leads Pryderi's hounds into a strange fortress. He goes after his dogs, against Manawydan's advice, and never returns. Rhiannon goes into the fortress after Pryderi and is also imprisoned. Finally, the fortress disappears, leaving Manawydan and Cigfa alone.

The pair try to live by making shoes, but things go as before so Manawydan buys wheat. They return to Dyfed where He plants the wheat but when the crop is ready to harvest, mice begin to eat it. Manawydan manages to catch one slow, fat mouse, and declares that He will hang it for stealing.

The next day, He makes a show of building a tiny gallows and preparing to hang the mouse. A bishop appears and offers him a large sum of money to spare its life. Through clever questioning and bargaining, Manawydan discovers that the "bishop" is a powerful magician who has been the cause of all their troubles, and the fat mouse is his pregnant wife. Manawydan carefully extracts promises that everything will be put right before handing the mouse over. Pryderi, Rhiannon and the kingdom of Dyfed are restored.

Perhaps it isn't easy to get a sense of who Manawydan *is* from this synopsis, but it might help to know that elsewhere in Welsh lore He is referred to as one of the Three Humble Chieftains of Britain, described as those who would not seek a kingdom, although it was theirs to take. This is because Manawydan should have inherited Bran's throne, but it was usurped while he and Bran were away fighting in the Second Branch. Manawydan chooses not to pursue His claim, which is not surprising as He is always counselling peace.

Of all the male characters in the Mabinogi, Manawydan seems the wisest, the most blameless, and the most peaceful. Because of this, He is a good deity to approach when you know you need these qualities or when you feel you could do with some fatherly guidance and protection. He shows us that even defending what you see as your honour is not always the wisest course.

Unlike Manannán, Manawydan, offers us no display of His own ability as an illusionist or magician. Instead, He shows great cunning at unravelling a strong and complex enchantment. If you are seeking insight into complex problems, or protection from magical interference, I can think of no better ally than Manawydan fab Llŷr.

MÁNI

Irisanya Moon

With so many Norse gods seemingly focused on battle and the trials of love, Máni offers a different perspective into the culture. As the personification of the Moon, Máni arrives into mythology via the *Poetic Edda*, as translated by Snorri Sturluson, and in the *Prose Edda*. Máni is often written about in relation to his brother the Sun, or Sol.

In the Henry Adams Bellows translation of the poem, *Voluspa*, there is a dead seeress (or volva) who speaks of the sun and moon.

"The sun, the sister of the moon, from the south
Her right hand cast over heaven's rim;
No knowledge she had where her home should be,
The moon knew not what might was his,
The stars knew not where their stations were."

It was common knowledge in the time of the Norse gods that the Sun and the Moon were chased through the sky by a wolf who was said to be protecting the woods. In some texts, it is said that some were jealous of the Sun and the Moon, so the two were placed into the sky.

Some give different names and qualities to Máni: lune, waxer, waner, year-counter, clipped, shiner, gloam, hastener, squinter, and gleamer. Additionally, some translations offer that Máni may have been in a relationship with a jotunn or a giantess.

Máni is the brother of the siblings, with Sol being the sister. Together, they ride through the sky in horse-drawn chariots as Skoll, the wolf, and Hati, Hate, follow them again and again. At the end of the world, the wolf will overtake them. In other theories, it is said that in the end of the word, Máni is the heavenly body that must be destroyed. When an eclipse happens, this is when the wolf has gotten too close.

To work with Máni is to work with the movement of the shadow, the waning and the waxing of a brilliant being in the sky. When you want to know Máni better, you call on him by going to the clear sky to watch him travel the length of a moon cycle. Though he is often spoken of in relationship to his sister, Máni also offers his own wisdom.

Some say that Máni is where the idea of the Man in the Moon originates. Seen as a being with dark hair and silver eyes, he serves the Aesir gods. He is also served by two child spirits – Bil and Hjuki who carry pails of water. While Bil decreases the water by pouring it out of the pail, Hjuki fills up the pail with water. Again, this relates to the energy of waxing and waning of the moon, and how it relates also to the tides and bodies of water.

Máni tells humans about time and about the passage of time. While not the moon, Máni is the one who guides the moon across the sky. He also was invoked in Scandinavia, Germany, and England for spellwork. In *Havamal*, Máni is related to both blessings and curses, while also being a protector of the dead and the living. He was also connected with seeing into the future, as well as with seidr practices of prophesy.

Many will work with Máni when they want to protect children or support vulnerable young ones. If you need to have extra help for children, he is the one you call on. Máni helps to protect and guide Bil and Hjuki, and is said to have rescued them from neglectful parents. In other sources, it is said that Bil and Hjuki were forced to carry water all night by a cruel father. With this in mind, you might call on Máni to help with strong protective magick for children and to guide you as you seek answers about what to do in the future about the children.

The moon and Máni are associated with helping with crop fertility, marriage, and love, anything that has cycles of increase and decrease. Some have also worked with Máni to help with financial gain and with planting or harvesting actions.

Some believe Máni to be older than any other gods, which would make sense as he is related to the moon. And while it would be easier to have a clear understanding of Máni, can we really pin down the definition of the moon?

While there isn't a lot of lore that survives in relation to Máni, he offers the wisdom of movement and cycles. He protects those who are vulnerable and he takes care of those who need extra care. Some resources note he helps those with emotional pain and mental illness, supporting them to have what they need and to know they are not alone. Perhaps all we need to know about Máni can be seen by looking to the moon, watching the fullness and the empty, and knowing we too can be chased and fierce at the same time.

MARDUK

Jo Robson

Marduk is of Assyro-Babylonian origin. He was the first son of Ea and Dankina the earth goddess. Marduk is a God of Spring, a God of Agriculture and the root of his name can be interpreted as calf of the storm – a storm god. He is also referred to as Bel in the old testament (Isaiah 46:1 and Jeremiah 51:44).

He is connected with Ishtar as one of her named consorts and also is known as husband to Zapanitu (Zerpanitum) (she who produces seed).

Although the Assyro-Babylonian pantheon remained fairly stable from an early date, different gods held ascendance which was much to do with the changing politics and ascendancy of cities in the region. Marduk as the patron of the city of Babylon rose in ascendancy as Babylon the city prospered. As principal deity Marduk embodied 50 other major deities becoming virtually the sole god.

Marduk plays a key role in the Enuma Elish (creation myth): In the beginning the primordial element was water, divided into Apsu (sweet water) of male gender and Tiamat (salt water) female in gender. By the mixing of these two beings was created Mummu (vizier of the gods) and Lakhmu and Lakhamu two serpents. The union of Lakhmu and Lakhamu produced the gods Anshar and Kishar. Anshar and Kishar came together and produced An who was the consort of Antu. The children of An and Antu included Ellil the god of air and Ea the god of wisdom, magic and the source of sweet water.

Ea and his brothers roamed across the waters which drew the attention and anger of Apsu and Tiamat. Apsu felt that the young gods should show respect and decided to act against Ea and his brothers. The brothers heard what Apsu intended and killed him.

Tiamat racked with rage and grief at the loss of her consort, Apsu, created monsters who were set against the gods for both Apsu's death and for their creation of winds which disturbed her great body. Ea, Anshar and An tried to destroy Tiamat and her monsters but failed. Marduk approached the three gods and vows to defeat Tiamat if they would then recognise him as king of the universe. The gods set Marduk a test to prove his powers over the sky, on passing the test he was recognised as the King of the Universe.

In his battle with Tiamat, he took the form of a warrior and using his thunderbolt and stirred the waters of Tiamat until she became a huge monster. After Marduk slew Tiamat he used her body to create the heavens and earth. An act changing the natural and chaotic creation process into a more ordered process. After creating the earth and constellations Marduk tasked Ea with creating humans from the bones and blood of Kingu – the chief monster and Tiamat's lover. Humanity would serve the gods, especially in Babylon where Marduk had his sanctuary.

The most important festival in the Assyro-Babylonian calendar was the Spring Festival in March which marked the first day of spring and was intricately linked with Marduk. The festival lasted for 12 days and started with four days of mournful prayers expressing the people's fears and doubts. Priests made daily prayers to the absent Marduk to protect Babylon and its people. At the end of the fourth day there was a recital of Enuma Elish and the king prepared himself to face the judgement of Marduk. On the fifth day the King submitted himself to judgement, stripped of his royal regalia he uttered a prayer to Marduk *"I have not sinned, Oh Lord of the Land, I have not been negligent to your divinity, I have not done harm in Babylon..."* During the recital a priest slapped the King before he was redressed in his finery. A symbolic act representing the decline of the state and its rebirth. Marduk then faces battle with the Ekimmu, evil gods of the underworld where he becomes trapped. On the seventh day his rescue is achieved by his son Nabu (who arrives on the sixth day to much rejoicing) and other protector deities from other major Babylon cities. On the eight day the gods convene to re-elect Marduk their leader. On the ninth day Marduk's likeness was processed from his temple to *bit-akitu* (festival house) through the Ishtar Gate along the processional way. On the tenth day Marduk holds a feast for the gods and then undertakes the sacred union with Ishtar (fertility rite). The eleventh day saw the gods meet in council to decide the fate of mankind for the upcoming year. The final day of the festival saw the gods returned to their temples. The people were reassured and armed to deal with any changes in the coming year before returning to work beginning again the agricultural year.

MERCURY

Rebecca Beattie

Working with Mercury is not for the faint-hearted. As if to demonstrate this, the first draft of the piece I wrote for this celestial messenger god vanished from my hard drive without trace. You see, Mercury is not only the ruling god of communication and travel, he is also the Roman equivalent of Loki, the trickster god. When you start working with Mercury, don't be surprised if arrangements go awry and things go missing – Mercury is after all the God of pickpockets, as well as banking and merchants. If you ask him to bring wealth to you, it will as likely vanish as fast as it arrived. If, however, you want to improve your trade, your divinatory skills, your eloquence, or your ability write well, then he is your God.

My relationship with Mercury stems back to the early days of my Wiccan training when we would exclaim in horror at the idea of the planet Mercury being in retrograde. Of course, the god and the planet are not the same thing, but they do share many elements in common (the planet being named for the God) and they share (mostly) the same correspondences in practical magic and herblore. If you work with the god Mercury or his planetary namesake, you will be calling on similar energies and with the same tools – his element is air, his day of the week is Wednesday (Mercredi) and his colour is orange. His herbs include lavender, bergamot, dill and parsley. The Mercury retrograde cycle — when the planet Mercury *appears* to be travelling backwards across the heavens — is a little more subtle than the popular press would have us believe. While areas ruled by Mercury may appear to be affected, it can also be a period of great introspection, and — depending on which astrological house Mercury is retrograde in — can lead to some interesting results.

Mercury is also the most fluid of the gods to work with, both in gender and in other aspects. In Greek mythology, his cousin Hermes was combined with Aphrodite to form the non-binary Hermaphrodite, and the German astrologer and magical practitioner Cornelius Agrippa also noted this mercurial aspect – he wrote that Mercury is the sovereign of animals *'that are of both sex and change sex'*. Mercury — the liquid element — was named for this quality too. It is no surprise we refer to those things that are erratic and unpredictable as mercurial. This god will keep you on your toes.

In Roman mythology, Mercurius was the son of Maia and Jupiter, but he was a late addition to the Roman pantheon when it was syncretized with the Greek religion, hence the frequent fusing of Hermes and Mercury. The festival of Mercuralia was celebrated on May 15th, when merchants would travel to his sacred spring at Porta Capena and sprinkle the water on their foreheads, their ships and their cargo. To begin with Hermes and Mercury were both depicted with the same winged shoes, helmet and the caduceus wand – the herald's staff entwined with two snakes which was gifted to him by the god Apollo. As the Roman empire spread across Europe, he then became merged with other European gods. While Mercury is placed firmly in the Roman pantheon, his quicksilver and fluid nature means I often work with him in the form of his many cousins and counterparts – Hermes in Greece, elements of Ganesha in the Hindu tradition, Papa Legba in the Dahomey, and of course (as previously mentioned) Loki. The most appropriate way to call on him is to light some orange candles, and make up an airy incense blend for him – a teaspoon each of frankincense resin, parsley and dill herbs, blended with some bergamot and lavender oils (four drops of each, since four is his number). And if you want to make him really happy, you can also read the Orphic Hymn aloud to him:

> *Mercury, draw near, and to my pray'r incline,*
> *Angel of Jupiter, and Maia's son divine;*
> *Studious of contests, ruler of mankind,*
> *With heart almighty, and a prudent mind.*
> *Celestial messenger, of various skill,*
> *Whose pow'rful arts could watchful Argus kill:*
> *With winged feet, 'tis thine thro' air to course,*
> *O friend of man, and prophet of discourse:*
> *Great life-supporter, to rejoice is thine,*
> *In arts gymnastic, and in fraud divine:*
> *With pow'r endu'd all language to explain,*
> *Of care the loos'ner, and the source of gain.*
> *Whose hand contains of blameless peace the rod,*
> *Corucian, blessed, profitable God;*
> *Of various speech, whose aid in works we find,*
> *And in necessities to mortals kind:*
> *Dire weapon of the tongue, which men revere,*
> *Be present, Mercury, and thy suppliant hear;*
> *Assist my works, conclude my life with peace,*
> *Give graceful speech, and me memory's increase*

MOT

Laurie Martin-Gardner

God of death, infertility, and drought, Mot ruled the dark chasms of the Canaanite underworld. Although we do not know much about Mot or his worship, texts discovered in the ancient city of Ugarit (in modern day Syria) provide a glimpse into the terrible figure of Death whose mouth was said to stretch from heaven to earth. Ruling from deep within the earth in his city, Hemry, Mot sat within a great pit, crushing and devouring anything that drew too close. His hunger was insatiable and any that ventured near his mouth, even gods, did not return.

Despite his loathsome nature and fearful office, Mot was often described as "the Beloved of El," "El's darling," and "the Hero." El, the Canaanite Supreme God, was Mot's father although how Mot earned such lofty titles has now been lost to us. Most of what we do know about Mot comes from a series of fragmentary texts known as the Baal Cycle.

Mot enters the Baal Cycle after the Storm God has defeated Yam, god of rivers and seas, and has been crowned King of the Gods. Many of the details are missing, but one interpretation is that Mot becomes offended by a dinner invitation sent to him by Baal. Refusing the invitation, and in turn refusing to acknowledge Baal as King, Mot declares, *"I alone am he who will rule over the gods."*

Baal had defeated the tempestuous Yam, but he fears the wrath of the God of the Dead. He sends messengers to Mot to pay tribute but is refused. Mot will not be sated until Baal himself is dead and the earth scorched. Baal knows he cannot defeat Death and agrees to deliver himself to Mot. Gathering his clouds, wind, storm, and rains (as well as his servants and swine), Baal goes to the mountain of Kenkeny and is consumed by Death.

Baal's body is later discovered by his sister, Anath, in the land of Deber. With the aid of Shapash, the Sun Goddess, she carries Baal back to the slopes of Mt. Saphon. There she buries her beloved brother in the sacred grave of the gods of the earth. El, upon hearing of the death of Baal, enters an intense period of mourning and gashes his cheeks and chest with a stone in his grief. Anath grieves as well, but her heartache soon turns to rage and she seeks out Mot. Ripping away his clothes, Anath demands that Baal be returned to her. Instead, Mot terrorizes Anath by describing to her how he had crushed Baal in his jaws *"like a lamb."* Anath withdraws, and the earth burns under the glow of Shapash. Without Baal, drought grips the land, and the earth is parched and cracked.

Months pass but Anath still longs for her brother. At last, she finds her revenge, killing Mot with her sword and then disposing of his body as if he were no more than grain, scattering his ground-up remains over the land and sea. At the same time, El dreams that the Storm God is still alive and sends Shapash to look for him. Shapash enters Sheol, the underworld, and returns carrying the resurrected Baal.

The newly revived Baal wastes no time in confronting and vanquishing Mot, who has also been restored, but the victory is short lived. Seven years later, Mot returns to destroy Baal. They fight with no clear winner until Shapash warns Mot that El will strip away his throne if he continues. Mot is fearful of El, who now backs Baal, and reluctantly bows to Baal and returns to the Underworld.

Having defeated both Yam and Mot, Baal embodied the continuity of life. Neither Yam's floods nor Mot's droughts could prevent life from returning. At the heart of the Baal Cycle is the promise of better days, more bountiful days, which was immensely important in a land that often suffered through disastrous natural cycles.

Mot, like his fellow Canaanite gods, eventually entered into the Jewish faith as well. The Hebrew word for death is "mot" or "mavet," and in many biblical verses Mavet is the personification of death (either as a devil or an angel), just as Mot was in Canaan. Habakkuk 2:5 describes Mavet as greedy and never satisfied, a description very similar to the one found in the Ugaritic Baal Cycle. Some scholars believe the story of Baal and Mot even inspired the Jewish tradition of Passover.

Despite being Baal's adversary, Mot (like Yam) was never considered an evil god. Instead, the drama of Baal and Mot helped the people of Canaan understand the periods of devastating drought they often contended with. Like death, Mot was neither good or bad but simply a force to be acknowledged and accepted.

NABU

Scott Irvine

Nabu is the original messenger god who laid down God's law for humanity converting from hunter-gatherer into city dwellers. He was the heir to the Anunnaki throne, a royal prince who was descended from the Serpent bloodline of gods. Nabu's father, the current King of the Universe, Marduk was the son of the great wizard and Lord of the Earth, Enki who was son of Anu who reigned over all of heaven and father to all the gods and goddesses who conducted their business within the 'civilised' human mind. Anu was the order born from the chaos of Mammu who was born from the union of the first powers of Apsu and Tiamat, the Father God and Mother Goddess of everything that exists.

What makes Nabu special is that he was a royal baby born from a human mother, an earthling queen connecting us by blood with the gods forever opening the way for other Anunnaki gods to take women as wives and had legitimate families with them. Marduk and Sarpanit soon begat two sons, Asar and Satu to manage Anu's kingdom on Earth. With all the attention and adulation, wealth and power that came with kingship, Satu grew jealous and in a drunken rage killed his elder brother, contained his corpse in a metal coffin and hid it in a marsh near to the mouth of the Tigris River. Asar's queen, Asta refused to give up hope when Asar disappeared without fathering an heir and relinquishing the royal bloodline to the evil Satu. After a long search, Asta found her husband's coffin, opened it and gave the corpse her breath of life long enough for her to be impregnated with the royal seed for her descendants to continue the royal line. Asta kept the birth of her son Horon secret from Satu until the young god was old enough to revenge his father's death, killed uncle Satu and reclaimed the crown for his father.

Losing both sons to each other, Marduk and Sarpanit needed another heir. Under Anunnaki law, Horon lost his right to inherit the divine crown of heaven for murdering the king to become king and without an heir; the crown would revert to Marduk's cousin the Moon God Sin. Horon was banished to the north east of Africa to live out his time with the people of the Nile. Nabu was born to deliver the human congregation to God and administer his great grandfather's rule on Earth. He acted as a CEO to our planet with an office both in heaven and on Earth. Nabu represented God in our world and his descendants became the priests that would spread God's word to the new city dwellers of the Babylonian Empire. He ensured the heavenly laws were upheld and those that disobeyed were severely punished. Temple taxes and sacrifices gave the priestly castes a very good lifestyle without much physical effort.

Farms needed to be worked; cities had to be built, temples and factories created, which in a desert environment took a lot of planning and organising. The roaming non-productive Stone Age people were encouraged to work for a living and earn a day's wage. Humanity needed to be educated into a civilised way of thinking and being. Nabu is credited for introducing the Akkadian language, a Semitic tongue that had deeper meaning and understanding to words and sentences; it was a language with imagination, with romance and drama, tragedy and comedy; poetry was born and stories became entertainment and inspiration. Nabu gave the world a bite of the apple of knowledge and there would be no turning back; the genie was out of his lamp. Annual spring festivals were introduced by Nabu that included a lamb that was sacrificed and its bloody carcass smeared on temple walls that ensured a fertile harvest at the end of summer.

All religions of today can trace their core beliefs to Nabu's dogma from his divine ancestors in fulfilling Marduk's/Enki's/Anu's wishes for humanity. The priests of Nabu bought enchantment and magic into the world of transformation, the realm of birth and life, of work, taxes and death. With the hierarchy and laws that comes with civilisation, Nabu expanded the human mind to produce masterpieces of art, music and writing; great thought, knowledge and wisdom could be expressed and debated. A new world of religious order of faith and commitment was developed where God oversaw everything from heaven and his priests upheld law and order on earth, organising humanity to feed and clothe themselves through farming and become useful in a civilised society on a journey of progress and new technologies to improve (and take away) life. Religion was born and was here to stay.

NUADA

Morgan Daimler

Nuada is one of the more significant members of the Tuatha De Danann yet he is, perhaps, overlooked in the modern pantheon. When people mention a king of the Tuatha De they tend to focus on Lugh, and likewise when the treasures of the Tuatha are mentioned the primary focus tends to be on the Dagda and his cauldron or Lugh (again) and his spear, yet Nuada was also a king of the Gods and also bore one of the treasures. Looking at his mythology reveals a complex and important deity that is worthy of respect today.

The Tuatha De Danann were not always in Ireland, but came

as settlers among several such waves of invasion. When they did arrive, they were led by Nuada who was the king of the Tuatha de Danann at the time and had been according to lore for seven years. He led the Tuatha De in battle against the Fir Bolg who were already in Ireland then and did not want to share any of their territory. A series of great battles were fought on the Plain of Pillars and while the Tuatha De Danann finally triumphed Nuada lost his right arm in the last battle when the Fir Bolg warrior Sreng severed his shield arm. The missing arm was replaced by the physician god Dian Cecht and the smith god Credne with one of silver that moved just like an arm of flesh. Nuada's most well-known epithet is Airgetlamh, silver arm, which comes from this.

After losing his arm the Tuatha De Danann chose Eochaid Bres for their next king even though his father was one of the Fomorians, a group who had long been present in Ireland and often oppressed the other groups inhabiting it. Bres was a poor king who allowed his father's people to lay heavy taxes on the Tuatha De Danann, who eventually rose up and rebelled against Bres's rule. Part of what enabled this rebellion was the restoration of Nuada's original arm by the healer Miach; no one could be king who wasn't physically whole since the land mirrored the king meaning that Nuada had been disqualified as king when his arm was lost but was able to lead again with its healing. Restored as king, Nuada led the Tuatha De after Bres was displaced and in the battle that ensued against the Fomorians who sought to restore Bres's rule. According to some stories Nuada ruled for 20 years after being healed, while others say that he was killed along with Macha at the battle against the Fomorians.

Nuada's father is Echtach, and Nuada himself has four sons Tadg, Caither, Cucharn, and Etaram the poet, as well as a daughter Echtge. We do not know who their mother was. Some scholars connect him to Macha who may have been his wife and who we do know in the second battle of the Plain of Pillars died at his side fighting against the Fomorian king Balor.

When the Tuatha De Danann came to Ireland they brought with them four treasures which each possessed magical properties. Nuada has the keeping of one of these treasures, a sword which once unsheathed no enemy could escape and no wound dealt by it could be healed. In the book The Lore of Ireland Dáithí O'hOgain suggests that the story of Nuada's arm being lost may have been rooted in an older myth where there was an accident with his own sword, or even possibly an intentional sacrifice. O'hOgain suggests that this may have been a sacrificial act of creation possibly connected to the forming of a river. This idea may play into wider ones which suggest that Nuada may also have been known by the names Nechtan and Elcmar; another epithet of Nuada's is Necht. This is only supposition but there are examples of deities with multiple names so it is possible. MacKillop agrees with this idea, connecting Nuada to both Nechtan and Elcmar, and from there further to the Boyne valley, the goddess Boinne (Elcmar's wife), and to Sid in Broga (Newgrange).

The meaning of Nuada's name is uncertain but there are different theories. O'hOgain suggests that it might mean catcher; Miranda Green favours the idea that the name may mean cloud maker and connects Nuada to British and continental counterparts such as Nodens, Nudd or Ludd, and Tyr. This idea is based on connections between the names in etymology and also similar mythic themes, particularly around losing a hand or arm. The idea of a god who loses an arm and has it replaced by one of silver seems to have been found across several Celtic cultures, supporting the idea of Nuada's wider importance and giving us other sources to compare his stories to.

Nuada is a deity of the cycle of kingship, honorable behavior, battle, justice, and possibly healing if we credit some of his wider associations. He may also be a god associated with rivers, particularly the Boyne, if we follow O'hOgain's theory about the older story of the loss of his arm and his connections to Nechtan. He has a lot to offer modern polytheists who reach out to him and seems very present today to those who seek to connect to him.

NJORD

Laura Bell

In Norse mythology, Njord is god of the seacoast, wind, sailing and fishing. He is part of the Vanir tribe of Gods, along with his daughter Freya and son Freyr, from his first wife Nerthus. The Vanir are the gods of prosperity, harvest and fertility and they were given to the Aesir as hostages to keep the peace between the waring Aesir and Vanir gods. There is evidence based on place names mainly in Norway and Sweden that show there were cults and worship of Njord. Those who worshipped Njord would likely have given thanks to Him for safe sea travel and for the fish that they caught. It is said that Njord was still being thanked by fisherman in Scandinavia as late as the 1800s for bountiful catches. He is honoured today in modern Heathenry and is fondly thought of as being a generous, diplomatic and fatherly god.

Perhaps Njord's most famous myth is about his unsuccessful marriage to Skadi. The most common version of this myth is as follows: The Norse gods had killed Skadi's father, the giant Thiazi, after he kidnapped the goddess Idunn. When finding out her father had been killed, Skadi, filled with rage put on her armour and gathered up her weapons and made the journey to Asgard to seek revenge for her father's death.

The gods offered her compensation for killing her Father and Skadi eventually agreed, one of her requests was that she wanted a husband. The Gods agreed to this, but they made a request of their own, she could only have one of their gods as a Husband if she chose him by looking at his feet. The gods lined up behind a screen and Skadi choose the cleanest, most lovely pair of feet. Surely these feet belonged to the beautiful god Baldur, Odin's son!? However, the feet she chose were Njords.

The couple agreed to get married, but because they were both unwilling to leave their homes, they decided to spend nine nights at Njord's home Noatun and nine nights at Skadi's home Thrymheim. However, Skadi despised Noatun, with its crashing waves and screeching sea birds. And when they tried to live together at Skadi's home, Njord hated the biting cold and howling wolves. Neither were willing to compromise their beloved homes and so they agreed to amicably separate, for they were as different as Summer and Winter. Something I take away from this myth is that even though Njord is a kind, mediating God who wants to keep the peace, he still spoke up when he was unhappy. The couple tried their best to make the situation work, but ultimately it wasn't worth sacrificing their happiness when the marriage wasn't a success.

Njord is still a very relevant god to work with today. He can be called upon to calm winds for a safe sea crossing or to grant safe travel in general. Njord could also be asked to aid in problem-solving and with help mediating in quarrels or situations where people have differing opinions. He was known as a very wealthy and generous god, so in times of need, you could ask him for abundance.

We all honour the gods in different ways, but I thought I'd include a few ways I honour Njord. Of course, the most obvious way would be to visit the coast, but living a couple of hours away from my nearest beach I only manage to visit a couple of times a year. I must use my imagination and an altar to work with and honour Njord. This sacred space includes Shells, sea glass, the rune Laguz -- associated with Njord, beach-inspired ornaments/artwork and a bottle of sand and seawater which all bring me visually closer to Njord's energy. Here I say prayers, make offerings and meditate.

Other ideas for ways you can honour and give thanks to Njord could include Litter picking at the beach to keep it clean and safe for the next generation. Reducing your usage of single-use plastics – which end up polluting the sea. If you are financially able you could donate to charities that help coastguards and/ or those that look after our sea life/beaches. And the most obvious would be to leave a safe and natural offering to the sea in Njord's name.

I like to think that although Njord is not a 'war god' he still offers his protection in a more subtle way and like a lighthouse he guides us to solutions, compassion and peace of mind.

ODIN

Irisanya Moon

Odin, Óðinn, Woden, and All Father. The one-eyed mystery who wanders the land seeking knowledge and offering wisdom. But also, a Norse god of complexity, Odin is a being who is also wrapped up in modern day conversations and interpretations. The sources for information on Odin are conflicting, at best, and inspirational for many.

With names meaning inspired, raging, or mad, Odin is also linked to being a poet and one who offers beauty as much as he offers fury. Perhaps it was his madness that inspired poetry or the poetry that drove him mad. And there are various sources of Odin, some in where we might know Germany today or Iceland. It seems the All Father continues to beckon us to learn more about him – and perhaps know him better.

Odin is described as wearing black or blue, in alignment with the colors of mourning in Icelandic tradition. In many pictures and stories, it is said he arrives with a large hat and cloak with a hood. Both of these items help to hide the missing eye and to offer him a sense of protection from the outside world. He is said to have gray hair, possibly a beard, and the lines of age and experience.

What seems to be clear about Odin is that he was present in the beginning, in the creation of the world (according to Norse mythology) and the separation of the gods into the Aesir and the Vanir. He was there for the time of the great war and the time of battles. Valhalla is Odin's hall and it is where those who fell in battle were lain.

It is important to know that Odin is often looked upon as an evil being, one who perpetuates the patriarchy and who is harmful. However, it is also clear that some of these interpretations are just that – interpretations. Odin is also the one who goes to Freya to get the knowledge of the runes, in some stories. He is also the one who dresses up in women's clothing, who might be seen as queer in today's language, and who prophesies because he can contact female seeresses after their deaths.

Even as Odin begins to come into clarity, other texts and stories offer up additional possibilities. In some books, Odin is said to have gained the knowledge of the runes, not from Freya, but from offering one eye in return for the knowledge. For nine days and nine nights, in the *Havamal*, he hung upside down from the branches of Yggdrasil, allowing himself to be pierced by a spear, without food or drink. In the end of this ordeal, sacrificing himself to himself, he was able to have the magick of the runes.

Those who seek to work with Odin more deeply might want to tap into his associations with poetry. As the mad poet and the one who drinks of the mead of poetry, he is inspiration embodied. Whether poetry is associated with his madness or not, it seems fair to say that Odin is one who allows himself to be taken in by ecstasy. Some texts have him inspiring the berserkers to battle so they would feel no pain and fight for as long as was necessary.

In addition, Odin was related to all that battle brought to a civilization – death, glory, and sacrifice. He was the one who offered victory to whomever he chose – or not. He was the one who decided to help a side by coming to leaders in disguise to offer help or not. Those who wanted to do well in battle were quick to offer a libation to Odin.

For many, the relationship between Odin and the dead is one that calls. He held the wisdom of knowing how to speak to the dead and to help others by collecting the knowledge of the dead. Not only did he hold the dead in the halls of Valhalla, but he was also one who visited those who were buried in mounds.

Odin is also associated with the magick of seidr and the runes. Seidr was the practice of prophesy and the act of coming to the high seat to communicate with the dead. Odin was considered to be a practitioner of seidr, even though he was sometimes mocked as this was a 'woman's' role. By communicating with the dead of the questioner, Odin could give answers to the one asking questions, allowing them to learn from the other side.

At Odin's side were Huginn and Munin, a pair of ravens that would fly around Midgard, or the human world, to find out what was happening and relay that information back to Odin. Also known as Thought and Memory, these ravens often arise in images and depictions of Odin as more cunning ways in which Odin learns what needs to be known in order to do what needs to be done.

OGMA

Robin Herne

Celticists such as Mark Williams have pointed out that the Gaulish deity Ogmios would not, following the rules of linguistics, have become known as Ogma by the time that name first appears in Irish manuscripts. That said, there is a similarity of character between the two, certainly in their eloquence and use of language to enchant. Lucian describes a wall relief of Ogmios which he had seen in Gaul which showed the god as an elderly man wearing a lion-skin cape and leading happy followers by thin chains linking his tongue to their ears. Ogmios carries a bow and a club, which partly led Lucian to compare him to an elderly Heracles. The Irish deity bears a speaking sword, Orna, which he acquires from a defeated enemy, Tethra. Surviving records make no mention of bows or clubs, but lost accounts may have included them (his brother Dagda certainly has a wondrous club).

The 14th century book, *In Lebor Ogaim*, names Ogma as the inventor of the ogham alphabet which he conjures with the use of a dagger. It may well be that there was once an inspiring myth of the creation, but that it was unknown to scribes who recorded this book.

He is referred to by the titles Grianianech, the sun-faced one, and Trenfher, the strong man (which conjures up the rather circus-like image of the Gaulish figure in an animal pelt). Another appellation sometimes given him – and various others – is Milbél, the Honey-Tongued. His two sons are Delbaeth (Magical Fire) who went to become a king of the Tuatha De Danaan and Tuireann who became a consort of the fiery goddess Brigid and sire of three sons who feature in one of the great tragedies of Irish literature. Some sources credit Etain as his daughter, others suggest her as his consort instead.

In the story of the oppressive reign of King Bres various deities are made to carry out manual labour. The fact of this inappropriate deployment shows Bres' incompetence to lead. The burden given to Ogma is the gathering of firewood. Whilst this may just be a random menial job, it could instead be symbolic of the gathering of the woods – the eadha or woods of the alphabet – destined not for the education of the world but for the fire pit. Bres might here be echoing the book burning emperors of Ancient China, with the added cruelty that the figure usually in charge of collating knowledge is ordered to incinerate it.

My own experience of Ogma in meditation and ceremony is of a professorial force, grandfatherly and bookish. The elderly face of the late actor Peter Cushing often comes to mind in meditation, yet it would be a mistake to consider Ogma frail or doddery. In myth he battles and single-handedly defeats the ferocious leader of the Fomorians, Indech, using the discarded sword that once belonged to Tethra. He is a presence who lives and flows through beautiful words structured by the rhythm of mathematics (poetic metre). Knowledge for him is as sweet and luxuriant as warm honey stored in the hive, the collective mind of all living beings (not simply humans). Stories, poems, Socratic questioning, the flow of knowledge and words are like water for a fish – Ogma flows through them all.

Gnomic lines from the Song of Amergin refer to the cattle of Tethra, asking who calls them. A reference from the *Tochmarc Emire*, spoken by the warrior Cuchulainn, suggests that the cattle of Tethra are actually fish (making the ill-fated Fomorian a ruler of the oceans). Caitlin Matthews suggests that the cattle are actually the stars, suggestive of the link to navigation (as well as astrology and astronomy, united disciplines in the distant past). If the sword transfers to Ogma, do the cattle also change loyalty – making the bardic god the one on whom the cattle smile, be that fish or stars or something else?

One myth accounts that Ogma died in the battle against the Fomorians – killed by Indech just as he is dealing the death blow, but this strikes me as a later twist introduced to emphasise the passing of the old order preparatory to the arrival of the new. Prior to the war Ogma encounters the newly arrived Lugh and issues a challenge. Bookish Ogma prises up a hefty flag stone and hurls it a considerable distance. Lugh responds by throwing the stone back so that it lands in the exact spot from which it was taken. It could be said that Lugh proves his worth by following the feat of knowledge back to its source. Ogma is, to the core, a teacher, a veritable Dumbledore guiding his students through the forest of the ancient alphabet and its semiotic layers. Ogma shows how words have power, shaping and transmuting the realities in which we all live.

WSJR/USIR (OSIRIS)

Jennifer Uzzell

Wsir, known in the modern world as Osiris, is one of the best known of the gods of Ancient Egypt and yet also one of the most mysterious. Most of what we know of his mythology comes from allusions from the Pyramid Texts and a number of New Kingdom stele, or from the more narrative writings of Plutarch (45-120 CE) and Diodores Siculus (90-30 BCE) during the Hellenistic period when the mystery cult of Isis and Osiris was well established.

The name of Osiris does not appear in any inscriptions until the middle of the Fifth Dynasty (2494-2345 BCE) although one of the his most common epithets, 'Khenti Amentiu' or 'Foremost of the Westerners' ('Westerners', in this context, refers to the dead as the world of the dead was often associated with the west bank of the Nile, where the sun set.) is seen as far back as the First Dynasty. Osiris is also referred to as 'King of the Living', 'Lord of Love', 'Lord of Silence' and 'He who is Perpetually Benign and Youthful'. He is generally shown as a kingly figure with a green complexion, carrying a shepherd's crook and a flail. These attributes were later associated with the divine authority of the Pharaoh. He wears the white Atef crown of Upper Egypt embellished with two ostrich feathers, and is shown as a mummy below the waist. There are differing opinions about the origins and meaning of his name but it may well derive from 'wser' meaning 'powerful'. He is also sometimes depicted as the djed pillar, representing strength and stability. The Ba of Osiris ('Ba' here is best understood as power or force of personality) had its own cult at Mendes. This was represented as a ram headed deity and was worshipped under the name of Banebdjedet (The ba of the lord of stability).

Osiris is best known as the lord of the Underworld and of the dead but his cult was also strongly associated with fertility and the regeneration of vegetation and with the annual flooding of the Nile. There are many versions of the myth of his death, mostly from Hellenistic sources, and it is difficult to be sure which, if any, is the original. Most involve his murder at the hands of his brother, his dismemberment, and the search for the pieces by his wife and sister Isis. She bound them together (thus creating the first mummy) and conceived a baby (the Younger Horus) while he was in this liminal state between life and death. There was an annual festival at Abydos where a passion play was re-enacted and images of Osiris made from grain paste were used in rituals representing death and resurrection. These culminated in devotees eating cakes and so identifying themselves with his death and resurrection. Plutarch tells us that he was addressed in these rituals as *the Bread of Heaven by which men live.*

Worship of Isis and Osiris continued on the Isle of Philae until Justinian I destroyed the shrine in the Sixth Century CE.

PAZUZU: LORD OF FEVERS AND PLAGUES

Marie RavenSoul

"I, the one that drives out Evil and exits Fate, the house that I enter, Headache and Disorder may not approach and harass it."- Pazuzu

Pazuzu is a desert wind god from Mesopotamia known for his evil and good nature. The earliest text that mentions Pazuzu is dated around 670 B.C. The first image of him appeared in the royal tombs of Kalhu towards the end of the 8th century B.C. Many other images were found in Assyria, Babylonia, and in the west part of Iran.

The meaning of Pazuzu's name might be twofold. The Neo-Assyrian Pa-zu-zu occurs in a text from Tell Halaf and is explained as deriving from the Aramaic pezoza which means 'made of fine gold.' The second might be from the word pessu which in Babylonian meant 'halt' or 'dwarf.' This could be the reason he has very small legs on one amulet, and in the inscription calls himself a u-GU-u meaning 'cripple.'

Artifacts discovered throughout history reveal that Pazuzu was regarded as a god, not a demon, as he has often been labeled. An Israeli museum contains an image of Pazuzu with horns around the top of his head, just like the crowns that adorn well-known gods such as Ishtar. Additional evidence comes in the form of a carnelian seal. Its creator gave Pazuzu a headdress in the form of a crescent and put a ball-staff at his feet. Only revered gods received these items.

Pazuzu was a chief protector of pregnant women and babies. During her pregnancy, a woman would wear a Pazuzu amulet around her neck. These amulets, made in the first millennium BCE, were for protection against evil. He was also called upon to heal the sick. A ritual would be done over a sick person, and the healer would either fasten a representation of Pazuzu's head on the person's body, or the sick would hold it in their hands. This would take the evil out of the person and they would get well.

Pazuzu would protect households against evil forces. In return, he sought hospitality. People would make a shrine to Pazuzu and would display a statue of him in the front room or entrance of their home.

The following is the incantation written on the statue:

"I am Pazuzu, the son of Hanbu, king of the evil lilu-demons.
I ascended the mighty mountains that quaked.
The winds that I went amongst were headed towards the west.
One by one I broke their wings."

This was to make a statement to the harmful entities, was an affirmation of his identity, and showed his authority over the household. Weapons were also crafted with the head of Pazuzu on them to protect the fighter in battle and to secure a positive outcome.

Pazuzu's greatest enemy is Lamashtu, a malevolent goddess from Mesopotamia. She was believed to be a predator and was blamed for miscarriages. It was said that she attacked women before and after childbirth, and then would go after their babies. Pazuzu was invoked to protect women from Lamashtu.

Many deities of the past seem to disappear, and we don't hear about them anymore. Yet Pazuzu's name has continued to make an appearance in many different places throughout the years. He is most known for being the entity that possessed Regan in the movie *The Exorcist* and is one of the deities in *The Necronomicon*, a grimoire written by horror writer H.P. Lovecraft.

To the Demonolator and Satanist, Pazuzu is seen as a god, daemon, and protector. Some Demonolator's have him as their patron while others only have a periodic working relationship with him. Whatever the level of devotion one might have towards Pazuzu, he is revered as a deity in his own right.

To communicate with Pazuzu, burn a grey, brown, or black candle in front of his image and recite the following prayer. If you prefer, you can write your own.

Hail Pazuzu!
King of the wind Demons.
I honour you this night.
From an ancient civilization, you rise.

Your presence is too powerful to contain.
Vilified by many,
your truth will be revealed at the right time.
Lord of Fever and Plagues,
your enemies cower in your presence.
You stand guard over households where you are revered,
and protect women who carry the unborn within.
Thank you for your assistance.
Come!
I listen for your voice within the blustering winds.
Nema!

To keep the connection strong, wear Pazuzu's amulet around your neck and perform a daily devotional ritual. Pazuzu is as real today as he was in ancient times. He is fierce but will help those who are sincere and who call upon his name with reverence.

PEGASUS

Kris Hughes

Most everyone has some awareness of Pegasus, the winged horse of Greek myth, but for many He is no more than a fairy tale figure like the unicorn, or a decorative symbol on a logo. However, Pegasus has a surprisingly rich network of relationships with other deities, and associations with a diversity of skills and attributes.

The origin of the name Pegasus is open to debate. Hesiod, writing around 700 BCE, related it to a word for spring (of the watery sort), while another etymology connects it to lightening, but modern scholars are doubtful on both counts. Each of us must decide whether we consider Pegasus to be a deity or not. It's likely that the classical Greeks did not, simply because He takes animal form, rather than human. Some modern Pagans, like myself, will have a more inclusive attitude. It's also possible that Pegasus predates classical culture.

According to Greek myth, Pegasus is the offspring of Medusa and Poseidon. Medusa is best known as a gorgon, or hideous, winged, snake-haired monster, but later Greek authors portrayed her as beautiful, perhaps as a way of reconciling Poseidon's attraction to her. She was sometimes depicted as a centaur (a horse's body with a human torso). Poseidon, Himself, also had equine associations, possibly originating as a hippomorphic river deity. In Arcadian myth He took the form of a stallion and raped Demeter, while She was in the form of a mare. All this helps to explain why the mating of Medusa and Poseidon might produce a winged horse. Pegasus also had a twin from this union, a great warrior with a golden sword, called Chrysaor, occasionally depicted as a golden boar.

While the union of Poseidon and Medusa is described as rape, Hesiod still gives it a rather romantic gloss, *"in a soft meadow amid spring flowers,"* before going on the tell how the hero, Perseus, beheaded Medusa, causing the twins, Pegasus and Chrysaor, to issue forth from her neck. In another version of the story, Medusa is a priestess of Athena whom Poseidon rapes in Athena's temple. Angered at this desecration, Athena curses Medusa to take the form of a gorgon.

Pegasus had a wonderful talent. Wherever He struck the ground with His hoof, a spring would issue forth. The most famous of these was the Hippocrene Spring on Mount Helicon, which was associated with the Muses. These goddesses were the inspiration of all art, music and philosophy, according to Greek belief, and Pegasus became strongly linked to Mount Helicon, the Muses, and poetry. The Romantic poets of the 19th century revived this idea to the extent that Pegasus became synonymous with poetic inspiration. You can still visit the Hippocrene

Spring, today, and it would be a worthy place of pilgrimage for anyone devoted to Pegasus.

One version of the Pegasus myth has Athena taming Him on Mount Olympus, but Pindar, writing in the 5th century BCE, has a more interesting version. The hero Bellerophon, who was also sired by Poseidon, wished to capture Pegasus in order to ride Him. He approached the seer, Polyeidus, for advice. Polyeidus instructed him to sleep in the temple of Athena, in order to seek a dream. In his dream, Athena appeared to him and gave him a golden bridle with which to tame Pegasus and told him to sacrifice a white bull to Poseidon, "The Tamer of Horses". When he awoke, he found the golden bridle beside him.

Having tamed Pegasus, Bellerophon rode him into battle against the Chimera, and on other adventures. Finally, Bellerophon tried to fly up to Mount Olympus on Pegasus, but he never made it. Some say he fell from the winged horse's back, others that Pegasus threw him off because he had no right to approach so close to the gods. Zeus, however, welcomed Pegasus to Olympus.

Pegasus seems to have been an eager servant of Zeus, pulling chariots and carrying lightning bolts for Him. He lived in the stables on Mount Olympus until Zeus finally rewarded Him for His service by turning Him into a star, which gave us the Pegasus constellation.

Pegasus is surely due our thanks and honour today for bringing forth the waters which inspire the muses, for where would we be without their help? As a willing servant of both the gods and humans, He models the servitude that we observe in horses everywhere.

You might show honour to Pegasus by offering a word of thanks when you see His constellation in the night sky in autumn, or by helping to care for local springs and wells.

POSEIDON

Robin Corak

Arriving at the ruins of Poseidon's temple at Cape Sounion, Greece, I stood in awe of so many white marble columns still standing, overlooking the ocean. Suddenly, I heard a clap of thunder that was so loud it seemed to shake the ground beneath my feet. The sky above was full of ominous clouds and I got the distinct impression that Poseidon was not happy.

The importance of Poseidon to the seafaring people along the coast in ancient Greece can't be overstated. The sea provided food and made long distance travel and trade possible. The ancient Greeks therefore had a great deal of motivation for appeasing the god known as the "Earth Shaker". Perhaps best known for his trident and his horses, Poseidon was often portrayed in myths as passionate and capricious at best and cruel and narcissistic at worst.

I have always had a weird attraction to Poseidon. On the one hand, I have a strong connection to the element of water and its deities have always fascinated me. Yet, unlike the softer energy of Aphrodite, the intense energy of Poseidon filled me with trepidation. His most notorious myths-including that of Medusa didn't help.

Depending on which version of the myth you believe, Medusa either agrees to sleep with Poseidon or is raped by him in Athena's sacred space. Rather than punish Poseidon, the angry Athena punishes Medusa by turning her into a hideous monster with snakes for hair whose gaze will automatically turn others to stone. Ultimately, Perseus cuts off Medusa's head and gives it to Athena so she can place it on her shield as a weapon.

It is important to consider the societal beliefs of the time in which the myths were written. In addition, one must dig deep and sift through the symbolism to find the deeper meaning inherent in the myth. Poseidon and Athena are, in many ways, exact opposites. Whereas Poseidon is ruled by his passions, the logical Athena is portrayed as being somewhat cold. Here we have a classic case of the heart (Poseidon) vs. the head (Athena). Athena's punishment of Medusa is one of the rare acts in which she appears to be driven by her emotions and lashes out at Medusa in the heat of the moment. For once, Athena's heart overrules her head.

Earlier this summer, I visited one of my favorite beaches to connect with and better understand Poseidon. I walked to a quiet place and stated my intent. Within moments, the waves began slamming into the rocks with great force and I stepped back as I felt Poseidon near. I felt the same stern, strong energy I had felt in Greece and I was forced to admit that his presence evoked some feelings of fear in me. I respectfully acknowledged the power he possessed and it was then that Poseidon shared some of his lessons.

Far from being a heartless deity, Poseidon cares for and is protective of those who live within his realm. Poseidon offers freedom and teaches us to ask for what we need. He encourages his followers to claim their own sovereignty rather than waiting for others to give it to them. Poseidon teaches us to not define ourselves or our abilities based on the limitations imposed on us by others or by ourselves.

At the same time, Poseidon teaches us the importance of staying in touch with our emotions and balancing pursuing our heart's desires with self-control and compassion. Like the ocean, we possess darkness and depth and cannot be contained by artificial boundaries. Just like water, we have the ability to both create and destroy, to both nourish and neglect. It is incumbent upon us to never lose sight of the fact that we ALL have both powers within us. We must be fully honest and accountable if we are to live in authenticity and access the power that Poseidon offers.

Back at Cape Sounion, I tried to get a sense of what may have been causing Poseidon's discontent. To place some distance between myself and the many tourists milling around the ruins, I moved further off to a site overlooking the ocean so that I could better connect with Poseidon's presence. In our modern society, we typically take water for granted and resonate with the softer qualities of the ocean, its beauty, its peaceful energy, and the recreation it provides. With the exception of the occurrence of natural disasters such as hurricanes, we don't often consider the ocean's power and give it its due respect.

In my attempts to commune with Poseidon, I got the sense that the experience of hundreds of tourists visiting the temple ruins each day-often without really knowing the deity to which the temple was dedicated, only served to reinforce our unwillingness as a society to truly appreciate the power and value of the sea. With heartfelt respect, I offered my thanks to Poseidon and shared with him that I was there to pay my respects to him and to the power of the ocean over which he reigned. I gave a silent blessing and an offering. I turned to rejoin my family, I looked up to see the sun brilliantly breaking through the clouds like a beacon of light. I smiled as the grey clouds dissipated and I walked back to the temple feeling honored to have witnessed his presence.

QUETZALCOATL

Amie Ravenson

Mesoamerican deities don't seem to get much attention these days. Perhaps it's because of the Euro-centric view that anything important comes from English-speaking countries. Maybe it's because of the mass Christianization of people of Central American descent. Or maybe it's all those problematic human sacrifices. Whatever the reason, there are some really interesting deities and myths that we can explore from the numerous cultures that called these places home.

For example, Quetzalcoatl (from quetzalli "plumed" and cohuatl "snake") was worshipped by several different Central American cultures from the 1st century CE through the Colonial Period in the 16th and 17th centuries. For those keeping score, that means that for 1400-1600 years, the feathered serpent god was venerated. That's quite a run. Mentions of the feathered serpent deity show up in the Mayan, Olmec, Teotihuacan, Toltec, and Aztec cultures, as well as other smaller cultures, but he was named Quetzalcoatl by the Nahua people of Mexico and El Salvador sometime after the 10th century.

Centers of his worship have been found in Teotihuacan, Xochicalco, Cacaxtla, and Cholula, Cholula being the most important center of worship to the Aztecs and Nahua peoples. The Mayans worshipped him at Chichen Itza and El Tajin.

He was the god of the wind, air, learning, and was associated with the planet Venus and the dawn. He was also the god of merchants, and of arts and crafts. Since his iconography was often found in populated cities, he also became known as a god of civilization and culture. He was credited with gifting humanity with books, the calendar, and maize, and is sometimes credited with the powers of death and resurrection. He was a god of the people, comparable to Hephaestus, who brought humans fire, and Odin, who brought humans the runes. He was one of the most benevolent and easy-going of the Aztec deities according to some sources, only requiring one human sacrifice per year. Some sources suggest he accepted only animal sacrifices. To the blood thirsty Aztecs, this was unusual in a deity.

Quetzalcoatl was represented mostly as a feathered serpent until the 13th century, at which time he began to be represented more and more as a humanoid figure. He often wore a hat with a hat band holding gold and black feathers, flowers, and tools used in sacrifice. He was often shown wearing a chest plate that was fashioned from the cross section of a conch shell that showed the spiral inside. This was a symbol of the winds and storms that he was responsible for. In fact, he was often associated with the rain god Tlaloc, as winds and rains often accompany each other.

One myth relays the tale of how he created humanity from the bones of previous races that were killed in the destruction of worlds that existed before ours. He went to the underworld to retrieve the bones, used his own blood to reanimate them, and created this world's race of humans. So, he is also a creator god in addition to his other duties.

In other myths, Quetzalcoatl is one of four sons of the original creator gods, and is tasked (along with his brother Tezcatlipoca) with creating the world. The brothers fight, and that's why there have been four worlds. Each time they fight and one is overthrown, a new world is created.

Other sources cite the belief that Hernan Cortez was Quetzalcoatl come back to earth to take his throne, and that was why it was so easy for the Spanish to peacefully overthrow the Aztecs. However, all of these sources are Spanish in origin, not Central American, and can be seen as propaganda to bring home to Europe. Other sources associate Quetzalcoatl with the return of Jesus Christ, but there are similar problems in the credibility of such accounts.

To honor Quetzalcoatl today, we can decorate with his iconography from temples all over Central America. We can add the feathered serpent to our altars in reverence. We can also use images of opossums, conch shells, and maize, as all were sacred to Quetzalcoatl. Feathers, dried maize, and snake skins would be good to include on an altar for him. Offerings of Mexican chocolate or maize might be a little more appropriate and easier to obtain than animals for sacrifice. Another way to honor Quetzalcoatl is to support indigenous Native American and Central American causes. He has become the symbol for several movements, including the Standing Rock protest of 2016. As a god of the people, he is a living god, and is still being invoked in times of need.

So, take a look at Quetzalcoatl and other Central American deities next time you're comparing pantheons and myths. You might find some interesting commonalities and a richness of stories to draw into your own practice. Blessed be!

SET: STORM GOD OF ANCIENT EGYPT

Marie RavenSoul

"I establish the crown upon thy head, even like the Disk on the head of Amen-Ra, and I will give thee all life, strength and health."
– Set, Pyramid Texts

Set was one of the most ancient of the Egyptian gods. He was the focus of the Egyptian people's worship since the Predynastic Period. The earliest representation of Set was found on a carved ivory comb from the Amratian period (4500-3500 BCE). A storm god, he was associated with frightening events such as eclipses, thunderstorms, and earthquakes. The glyph that represents him is within the Egyptian words for confusion, storm, rage, illness, and turmoil.

Set was identified with many animals including the scorpion, crocodile, serpent, and jackal. It was believed that certain fish were sacred to Set, especially the Oxyrhynchus and the Nile carp. He often appeared with red hair and has been called the 'Lord of the Desert' and 'Ruler of the South.' His name has been translated to mean 'destroyer' and 'instigator of confusion.'

Ramesses II (1279-1213 BCE) revered Set and made him a national god, constructing a temple in his honour. The priests of Set cared for his statue in the inner part of the temple. They were responsible for its upkeep and daily rituals. Whoever wanted his assistance would only be allowed in the courtyard to place their offerings or make petitions for help. Many would pray to Set for power over the storms and to obtain control of the winds and desert.

The mythology surrounding Set is varied. He is said to be the son of Nut and Geb and the brother of Nephthys, Horus, Osiris, and Isis. He was born by ripping himself out of his mother's body. He had many wives including Nephthys, Taweret, Anat, and Astarte. He was bisexual. Set was regarded as a hero and benefactor who helped people and provided for them after they died. He became the god of chaos and war, and then after killing Osiris, he was known as the first murderer. Horus, who represented the sky during the day, wanted vengeance, so he fought Set who represented the night sky. Horus stole Set's testicles and Set tore out Horus's eye. It was believed that they would fight until the end of time when Ma'at was destroyed and Chaos reigned.

One of the most well-known myths regarding Set is when he protected Ra against Apep, a serpent of chaos and evil. As Ra's barge descended into the underworld, it was attacked by Apep who wanted to kill Ra. Set defended him by stabbing Apep with his spear.

Set was associated with Typhon by the Greeks and then the Devil of Christianity. This was because of his association with darkness, and because he was cast out of the home of the gods for rebelling against the established order.

In the present day, Set is still revered by many people and is mentioned in literature, video games, movies, television, and music. In 1975, Michael Aquino, a former high-ranking member of the Church of Satan, performed a ritual to Satan. He was told that Satan wanted to be called Set, his true name. Aquino founded The Temple of Set, an organization that reveres Set as a real spiritual entity. It encourages the development of the individual whose goal is to 'come into being,' the Egyptian hieroglyphic term being 'Xeper.' It teaches that Set gave humanity individual self-consciousness or what is known as the 'Black Flame.'

Followers of Kemetism, a resurgence of the Ancient Egyptian religion that began in the 1970s, worship Set as part of their pantheon of gods. Their worship involves prayer and maintaining an altar with candles, statues, and offerings.

Theistic Satanists view Satan and Set as being the same entity, both names being used interchangeably. It is a very personal path as each Satanist relates to Set in a unique way.

To establish a connection with Set, light a black candle in front of his image and say an invocation prayer. You can use the following one or write your own.

Hail Set!
Ancient One.
Master of storms and Lord of the Desert.
Worshipped by the Ancient Egyptians.
Oil and incense they offered you.
Bowing before your image they sang hymns of adoration.
You bestowed upon them many gifts.
Gave humanity self-consciousness.
In this present age,
your power is evident throughout the world.
Come!
Come join me this night.
Teach me your mysteries,
as I worship at your altar.
I honour you.
So, mote it be.

SHIVA

Raegan Shanti

Within the Hindu Pantheon, there is a central Trinity which hold the balance of the world within their hands; the Creator, Brahma; the Maintainer, Vishnu; and the Destroyer, Shiva. This paradigm is a very simplistic way of describing these Gods, as their roles are far more complex than that. A quick look at these descriptors, especially through Abrahamic eyes (for example), would give you the impression that Shiva is a demon of sorts, tearing through the world and creating chaos. This couldn't be further from the truth.

Within Hinduism, and perhaps even Indian culture itself, destruction is a considered a necessity of life: for new things to happen or grow, the previous must be destroyed. For a fruit to come into being, the preceding flower must wilt and die. For a soul to be reborn, the previous self must be destroyed. Shiva represents the necessity of shedding the old and welcoming what is to come.

Shiva, like most Hindu Gods, is depicted with blue skin to show his Divinity and, in many paintings, he is depicted as sitting cross-legged and holding up his hand in a position (or *mudra*), known as Abhaya-mudra, which means "do not fear". His flowing hair is partly tied in a bun, from which the water of the Ganges flows down, and he is adorned with animal skins, which symbolise his ability to conquer all foes, regardless of their strength. He is also often depicted with his animal companions: Nandi the Sacred Bull and Vasuki, the world's first cobra.

Another common depiction of Shiva is as Shiva-Nataraja, or Lord of the Dance. This bronze statue shows him dancing the sacred Tandeva, which keeps the Universe in balance. In this dance, he has defeated the demon of Ignorance and brandishes Agni, the Sacred Fire, and Damaru, the drum from which comes the heartbeat of the universe.

First and foremost, Shiva is a protector God. This standing goes all the way back to the beginning of the world in Hindu mythology, the very beginning of the universe was nothing. The sound of Aum (Om) filled the space and void, developing into a power from which came Brahma, Vishnu and Shiva. Brahma dreamt the world into being, along with seven wise men, from whom spawned the world's Gods and the world's Demons.

A curse befell the Gods, causing the fights between them and the demons to swing quickly in favour of the demons. The gods went to Vishnu for help, and he proclaimed the only way to reverse the curse was to partake of the ambrosia, which lay in the depths of the Milk Ocean, which would need to be churned. The Milk Ocean was indeed an ocean of great size, and no instrument was big enough to churn it so, upon Vishnu's suggestion, the gods uprooted the mountain, Mandara, and called upon Vasuki to help. He wrapped his body around the mountain and the gods used him as a lasso to churn the milk.

The Milk Ocean solidified and produced the moon, the stars, the Sacred Cow, the Goddess Lakshmi, among many others. What lurked underneath, however, was a malicious blue mist filled with poison. It rose from the ocean's depths and entwined itself through the gods, through the Heavens, through the underworld, through the world itself. It choked everyone within its grasp.

Vishnu called out for Shiva, who appeared and attempted to swallow the poison and save everyone by sacrificing himself. Refusing to let her partner die, the Goddess Parvati grabbed him around the neck and prevented the poison from travelling further than his throat. The ambrosia was recovered and the curse was undone. One of Shiva's many names is Neelkantha, which means "the blue throated one", referencing this story.

Shiva is frequently depicted with the Ganges flowing from his hair and the river itself is the most sacred one in Hinduism.

Shiva was there at its birth, when it was blessed to the human race by Brahma. However, the force of the water was far too much – it eroded land, flooded crops and destroyed houses. The gods tried to stem the flow, but it was out of control. Shiva arrived to save the day – as the water began from the Himalayas, Shiva laid his head across where the water ran and, as it flowed through the bun at the top of his head, the water calmed and began to flow much more gently. He left his hair there in the form of a large stone called *Kush*. Above the Kush, the River Ganges flows wildly but after it, the water flows smooth.

In all of his guises, Shiva is a force to be reckoned with, but never one to be feared. His role is to destroy obstacles, protect the Earth and keep the Universe in perfect balance with his dance.

TATQIM

Heather Dewhurst

Tatqim is an Inuit God of the Moon, hunting and reincarnation. The moon is his partially burned out torch that he carries to light his way as he constantly and lecherously chases his sister, the sun Goddess Seqinek. The story of how They came to be the Moon God and Sun Goddess demonstrates a little of the way of life lead by the Inuit people, as well as the beliefs that were important to them

As children, Tatqim and Seqinek grew up together, playing and loving each other as brother and sister. When They came of age, they were separated, He to the male camp, Seqinek to the female and were not allowed to see each other for several years. One day, Tatqim climbed to the top of the hill that separated the camps to look at the women, there He saw the most beautiful of them all and lusted after her, not realising She was His sister. After watching this maiden for a few days, Tatqim saw a way into the women's camp and that night He crept in, found where she was sleeping and forced Himself on her, running off afterwards!

Seqinek was distraught, but came up with a plan to trap her assailant, so that night She covered Her body with soot from the fire. Sure enough, Tatqim came to Her that night, again running off. The next morning, Seqinek went with her elders to the male camp, where they found the only man covered in soot. Seqinek, realising it was Her brother who had raped Her, became even more distressed and taking a knife cut off Her breasts before running away from the tribe.

Tatqim was so ashamed at what he had done, especially as incest was strictly taboo, that He chased after Seqinek, following the trail of blood She was leaving, all the time shouting how sorry He was, but She did not stop until nearly all the blood had left Her body. Tatqim found Her and cradling Her in His arms begged her not to die, telling Her that He would do anything to make up for His wrongdoing towards Her. With Her final breath Seqinek forgave Him.

At that moment, the older Gods who had been watching from Their home in Udlormiut, saw the love each had for the other and decided that each would rule part of the day, but not together, bringing light and providing food from crops as well as the sea with the tides, for the Inuit people.

Although They were never meant to be together again, there is a story to explain how solar eclipses come about. One night just before He was at His full radiance, Tatqim overheard some Inuit men planning to shoot the Sun, Seqinek, from the sky because She had been too hot, and their crops might spoil. The next day, He altered His path so that He could come to stand in front of Seqinek and protect Her! However, another story has it that as Tatqim continues pursuing his sister on daily basis, She lets Him catch Her and these occasional couplings are the eclipses.

In addition to His role as Moon God, He plays a very significant role in the Inuit cycle of reincarnation. When human and animal souls in the afterlife are ready to be reincarnated, the Goddess Tapasuma instructs Tatqim to transport them to Earth, further instructing him what type of life form each soul should be reborn as. Tatqim takes these souls to Earth in his divine dogsled pulled by four huge dogs (or just one huge dog in some stories), when He is undertaking this role the night is moonless.

In the folk tales, it is Tatqim who created vaginas and anuses. The story of this is that long-ago animals did not have either orifice, which meant that the disembowelling Goddess Ululijarnaq, would take her knife to carve babies or waste matter out of people's insides as needed. Tatqim saw how inefficient that was, so took His hunting knife and cut vaginas into all female life forms and anuses into all living things. The Inuit believed that was why women bleed each month, from the wound Tatqim had given them. This association with the vagina is thought to be how the Moon God got His reincarnation duties, as the vagina is the portal through which animal life enters the world. Women hoping to conceive would pray to Tatqim for children, believing that sometimes He would come down and impregnate them personally.

THOR

Andrew Anderson

Thor (written as either Þórr or Þunarr in Old Norse) is the God of thunder and protector of mankind who was, and remains, one of the most popular deities from Norse mythology. He is the son of Odin, the chief God in the Norse pantheon, and the Goddess Jord, whose name translates as "Earth". The mythology presents Thor as a God of many contradictions. For example, Thor is sometimes presented as a tactician, out-thinking his enemies, while at others he can appear oblivious and is duped by fairly obvious, although primarily magical, means.

The tone of the mythological tales about Thor also vary greatly, with some being broadly comic and others far more serious, even apocalyptic. This sense of contradiction can also be seen in some of Thor's associations. Such as he was often called upon at weddings to help bless the couple with abundant fertility, while he was also invoked as part of funerary rites. Part of his continuing popularity stems from the belief that Thor was a God of the Common Man. This was exemplified in his choice of transport. Thor is often described as walking or travelling on a chariot pulled by goats rather than on a horse.

This sense that Thor was somewhat grounded could well be the reason why his name often appears in both place and personal names from the periods, alongside accounts of a large number of shrines built in his honour. Many people today come to Thor through his appearance in the popular Marvel comics and films, although the references to him in the Sagas and both the Prose and Poetic Eddas give a different sense of Thor from the one presented in the media today. A small but pertinent example of this is that, in the ancient texts, Thor is often described as having red hair and a beard, rather than the blonde hair we see presented on screen today.

In mythology, Thor is often presented as being of enormous size and strength, which accounts for his ravenous, barely satiable appetite. In the Prose Edda, for example, Thor even eats his own goats, Tanngrisnir and Tanngnjóstr, although he does keep their skin and bones so he can resurrect them the next morning to pull his chariot. While many of the written accounts of Thor come from Iceland, with obvious links to wider Norse culture, Thor's influence stretches beyond Scandinavia to countries such as Germany and Britain. For example, echoes of Thor can be found in the Germanic God Donar, while among the Anglo-Saxons, Thor was known as Thunor, giving his name to the fifth day of the week, Thursday.

Thor, like many other thunder Gods, is associated with the

Oak tree possibly because Oak trees are commonly struck by lightning. Thunder and lightning itself has often been seen as a signifier of Thor's presence, either rumbling over head as he drives by in his chariot, or as a sign that he is using his hammer, Mjölnir, an incredibly powerful and potent tool which is shown in the mythology even to be capable of reshaping the landscape and knocking down mountains. The hammer will be inherited by Thor's sons, Magni and Modi, upon his death, with Modi surviving Ragnarök to assume his father's protective role.

Generally travelling alone, Thor is sometimes accompanied by the human Thjálfi, but also by the trickster deity, Loki, who generally creates trouble which the God of thunder has to unravel. For example, in the poem Lokasenna, Loki claims to have slept with Thor's wife, Sif. There are many stories of Thor fighting giants and, as such, he has become known as something of a giant killer. However, in other stories, Thor is shown as having allies amongst the giants and is seen to kill other dangerous beings, such as trolls and dwarves so his reputation as an enemy of the giants has been overstated. Loki's child, Jormungandr, otherwise known as the Midgard Serpent, is often portrayed as Thor's chief enemy, and they fight on several occasions. The pair will undertake their final battle at Ragnarök when Thor will finally kill Jormungandr, but will himself be fatally wounded and die as a result.

It is interesting to note that Thor's popularity remained through the period of conversion to Christianity, where one tale tells of another potential battle, this time with Thor challenging Christ to a fight! Thor has also become one of the primary deities in the modern Heathenry movement with pendants of Mjölnir becoming a symbol of faith. Thor's popularity continues to grow in the twenty-first century.

THOTH

Dorothy Abrams

Thoth, also known as Djehuti, holds the Universe together by its orbits, systems, galaxies and all the created space. He is self-created in many accounts or born of the head of Set from the seed of Horus in others. Roughly correspondent to Hermes and by extension Mercury, he is called Hermes Trimegistus or Thoth the Thrice Great. His seat is Hermopolis. Still acknowledged in art and education he appears on the logo of the University of Cairo holding a stylus and tablet. That depiction recognizes Thoth's creation of writing and magic, the art of spelling being a magical skill. Along with the art of magic and spell making Thoth encompasses the wisdom and power of the moon. He can be celebrated as a Moon God along with Khonsu with whom he marked out time with the moon phases.

Depending on one's understanding of the origin of Thoth, his family relationships can recognize Isis as his grandmother or he as her creator. Two Goddesses identified as his wives are Ma'at and Nehmetawy. Ma'at and Thoth are guardians on either side of the solar boat of Ra as he traverses the sky. Thoth protects Ra from the serpent which attacks the boat as it passes through darkness. Ma'at and Thoth are both judges of our souls after death. Ma'at balances the soul with a feather to weigh its purity. Thoth oversees the integrity of the balance as the ultimate champion of even handedness. Nehmetawy is associated with Hathor and Seshat and may be different aspects of the same Goddess since all appear as partner to Thoth and share in offering wisdom and intervention when her celebrants are in trouble. Seshat is the goddess of writing, books, libraries and librarians. Hathor is a primordial Goddess of love, the arts which include the literary arts, and motherhood.

Thoth was sent to retrieve the eye of Ra from the Distant

Goddess, daughter of Ra who disappeared into the wilderness after a dispute. She was too powerful to be ordered, so in his animal forms Thoth persuaded her return so that the solar eye was restored. His reward was his wife Nehmetawy who is the Distant Goddess won over to reason.

Thoth is also a gambler and the possessor of the secrets of magic and science which are recorded in the secret Book of Thoth. Together with Khonsu Thoth marked out time through the night and day setting a year at 360 days. As it happened, Nut the sky Goddess was forbidden by Ra to birth children on any day of the year. To aid Nut Thoth engaged in a game of senet with the Khonsu whose light was a balance to the sun and Ra. Thoth wagered his secret knowledge. Khonsu wagered moonlight. The games went on and on until Thoth won enough light from the Moon to create 5 extra days outside of the 360 day calendar. During those times, Nut birthed the children conceived with her husband Geb: Osiris, Horus the Elder, Set, Isis and Nephthys.

Thoth also had notable children. Together with Nehmetawy he fathered the 8 ancient ones known in Hermapolis in the Middle Kingdom as the Ogdoad. However, the first references to them in the Old Kingdom were in the dim recess of memory, so much so that they were nearly forgotten concepts of universal powers. They were never clearly defined though later priests attempted to do so. Suffice it to say the Ogdoad, 4 pairs of males and females, express their father's ordering of the universe and life forces with science and magic which are likely tucked away in The Book of Thoth.

There are two main sacred animal associates with Thoth. As the ibis headed God, Thoth created other deities with an egg laid in the Milky Way. Alternately Thoth's egg was the Cosmic Egg which hatched the universe. The ibis is a liminal bird, treading between water and solid ground. It is a source of wisdom and a measurer of universal proportions in that its stride is the sacred cubit known in the ancient world for the length of a man's fore arm or about 18 inches.

The second animal correspondent is the baboon, a keeper of equilibrium. Again, the dog-faced baboon is an animal that balances the universal times and measurements. It represents intelligence. A steady gaze from a baboon measures the individual. As such the baboon epitomizes Thoth's role as judge of the dead. The God could appear as a human with the animal head or as the animal. He will still visit his students in ordinary reality in those forms, though those living in places without either baboon or ibis may find his instruction through certain canines and herons. These are not perfect substitutes but Thoth does what he will.

In summary, we seek the face of Thoth in times needing justice or balance. We ask for inspiration in the written word as reader or author. We study the interconnections of time, space and universal proportions under his tutelage. At the root of all these ideas is magic: the magic of science, of the unexpected and the transformative. Thoth stays with us from the cradle to the grave and beyond in the next world.

TSAO WANG

Ness Armstrong

You will find him hanging above the stoves of many a Chinese household – not literally of course! But a paper effigy, the image of a friendly looking man, looking down on the kitchen where he resides, watching over the family and making observations on what has been said and done over the course of a year. Sometimes the image is just of him, in other depictions, his wife is sitting next to him and it is she that takes down the notes for him.

This Stove God, or Kitchen God is known by many names

– Tsao Wang, Zao Jun, Zao Shen or Tsao Chun and he is a very important domestic God that protects the hearth of the home and the family that live within it. He is responsible for their happiness and their good fortune but this isn't given freely.

Over the course of a Lunar Year, Tsao Wang watches over the affairs of the family – what they do and say – what their values, morals and behaviors are – and all this is noted firmly within his memory and written down by his wife and stored away until a week before the Chinese New Year or the 23rd day of the 12th Lunar month. This is a very important time for the family, for this is when Tsao Wang will ascend to heaven to verbally deliver his report on the family to the Jade Emperor (also known as *Yu Huang*) – who is one of the most important Gods in Taoist tradition. Taoism is a Chinese philosophy that signifies the true nature of the world. Their thoughts and beliefs focus on genuineness, longevity, health, immortality, vitality and they live in harmony with nature and the universe.

During the course of the year while Tsao Wang watches over the family, many devout households will make offerings of food and light incense to honour him. This is done regularly on the 1st and 15th of the month but also on his birthday which is on the 3rd day of the 12th lunar month and most definitely on the 23rd day of the 12th lunar month.

The contents of Tsao Wang's report will determine whether the Jade Emperor rewards or punishes the household. If the Jade Emperor is pleased with the report, he will instruct Tsao Wang to increase the prosperity and happiness of the household. If the report isn't very favourable, he is instructed to withdraw both the happiness and the prosperity. Prosperity didn't just mean the riches of the household; it also refers to the comfort and wellbeing of the family. This includes protection of the household and the warding off of evil spirits too!

As the end of the Lunar year approaches, each household wants to make very sure that Tsao Wang delivers a good report when he goes to visit the Jade Emperor.

It is at this time that the family members of the household offer a sacrifice to Tsao Wang. It is called a sacrifice or offering, but it is more than likely considered a 'bribe'.

A sticky cake made with glutinous rice flour, sugar or honey called *Nian Gao* is one of China's traditional candies and is very often baked for Chinese New Year. Some of this very sticky cake is smeared onto the lips of Tsao Wang, which is said to either seal them shut or to sweeten them. This is so he either can't give the full report of the families' actions or spoken words or that he is bribed into giving a 'sweetened' version of it to the Jade Emperor.

In order to help Tsao Wang on his way to deliver his report, the paper effigy is taken down and burned. It is carried into the families' courtyard very carefully, ensuring that it faces south. Wealthy families placed the paper effigy into a palanquin. Silver paper money was put in front of it and final prayers were said to ensure that Tsao Wang delivered a good report. Firecrackers are lit to speed up Tsao Wang's journey and the rising smoke from the burning effigy signifies his ascent to heaven.

Some households have a statue of him which is taken down and cleaned instead. It is also at this time that the family have a house cleansing and garden tidy up in preparation for the New Year. With Tsao Wang away, the household took full advantage of not having his watchful eye over them and this was a time to indulge in merriment, gambling or other such pleasures that were frowned upon by the God. Seven days after Tsao Wang was sent on his way, it is time for him to return. The family welcome him with more offerings of food, more firecrackers are set off and a new picture of Tsao Wang is hung above the now clean stove for the year ahead.

TSUSANOO

Melusine Draco

Tsusanoo is the bad boy of Japanese mythology, infamous for his mischievous and sometimes destructive behaviour and has a reputation as being something of a trickster. Also known as Takehaya-Susano'o-no-Mikoto, he is the Shinto god of the sea and storms, and the brother of Amaterasu, the goddess of the Sun, and of Tsukuyomi, the god of the Moon.

The god was born when his father Izanagi washed his nose in the river when performing ritual cleansing rites following his experience in the underworld: which may explain why he always has a hint of 'darkness' about him. Initially, Tsusanoo ruled the *Takama no Hara* (High Celestial Plain) with his sister Amaterasu but from the very beginning, he caused trouble by destroying forests and mountains and killing local inhabitants down on earth. For this reason, he was banished from heaven. On the pretext of saying goodbye to his sister, Tsusanoo once again caused great destruction on his way to her palace that the mountains trembled in his wake.

Amaterasu was immediately convinced her brother was up to no good but when challenged he claimed he merely wished to bid her farewell and to prove his good intentions, said that if he could miraculously bring into the world five new deities and if they turned out to be male, it would prove his honesty. Tsusanoo then took the 500-jewel necklace of his sister, ate them and spat them out as a mist from which five male deities were born. These new gods or *kami* – along with the three female gods produced when Amaterasu performed a similar feat by eating her brother's sword – became the ancestors of the Japanese nobility.

Fueled by testosterone at having won his challenge, Tsusanoo went on another wild rampage. Once again, trees were destroyed and many rice-fields. Then, to add insult to injury, in a rather tasteless joke Tsusanoo flayed a divine horse and threw it through the roof of the palace where Amaterasu was quietly weaving. Furious at her brother's outrageous behaviour, the sun goddess shut herself in a cave and only came out again after much myth-creating enticement from the other gods, Tsusanoo was once again exiled from heaven. In some accounts he took up residence with his mother Izanami in Yomi, the underworld; while in other versions he rules the realm of the seas.

Descending to the earthly realm, Tsusanoo landed at Tori-kami in the province of Izumo and whilst wandering along the river he found three people weeping – an old man and woman and their beautiful young daughter – all sobbing uncontrollably and absolutely terrified. On enquiry, they told the god that their distress was caused by a gigantic serpent (known as Yamato-no-Orochi or the Koshi) which came to terrorize the region every year and ate one of their daughters and now the distressed parents were down to their last daughter, Kusha-nada-hime.

Never one to miss a trick, Tsusanoo struck a bargain with them that if he killed the monster, he could marry the beautiful girl. Agreeing to this, the parents followed the god's instructions and placed eight vats filled with extra strong sake at each of the doorways of their house. After a while, the monstrous serpent duly arrived with fire spitting from each of his eight heads. When the fearsome creature smelt the sake, it could not resist and each head drank from one of the vats. Consequently, the serpent collapsed completely drunk and Tsusanoo nonchalantly stepped out from his hiding place and lopped off each of the serpent's heads with his sword. Then opening the creature's belly, he discovered the special sword, the Kusanagi or 'grass-cutter' (in other versions of the story he extracts it from the serpent's tail). This sword, he presented to his sister (no doubt by way of apology for his earlier conduct), who gave it to her grandson Ninigi, who was the first ancestor of the Japanese imperial family. It became a part of the imperial regalia, preserved in the temple of Atsuta near Nagoya.

In the way of all gods, there are both the positive and negative features at the base of this god's character. From earliest times he was the god who was supposed to bring sufficient rain for the crops, which suggests his worship was derived from the priests performing rites for rain at shrines where sacred rice and water were regularly offered to the gods. Despite his reputation as a bad boy amongst the Shinto gods, Tsusanoo is credited with giving certain cultural gifts to mankind, including agriculture.

In Japanese art, Tsusanoo is most often depicted with wild hair blowing in the winds, wielding a sword and fighting the eight-headed monster Yamato-no-Orochi; he also plays an important role in modern on-line gaming as a sort of anti-hero.

TYR

Imelda Almqvist

↑ Týr er einhendr áss
ok ulfs leifar
ok hofa hilmir.
Mars tiggi.
Tyr is a one-handed god,
and leavings of the wolf
and prince of temples

A colleague of mine once joked in a Seidr class we co-taught that if there was such a thing as the "school disco" in our relationship with the gods, then I would be stepping out with Tyr!

To some this seems an odd choice. Tyr is often presented as a mysterious and less important or less prominent god in the Norse collective (it is debatable whether we can call this a pantheon, the reality of life in Viking and Medieval Northern Europe may not have been as coherent as that). In this short essay I will present two windows or lenses of perception on Tyr and both fascinate me equally. I will call them "arrows" because Tyr's rune looks like an arrow pointing up!

First Arrow

The Old Norse word Tyr just means "god". For instance, the god Thor is also called *reidatyr* or *the riding god*: the wagon god travelling the sky in his wagon (holding his famous hammer Mjølnir). The Old English variant is *Tiw*. Before Tyr, as we know him today, there was an earlier proto-Germanic deity called *Tiwaz*. The T rune in the Elder Futhark still bears his name: Tyr or (more commonly) Tiwaz.

Tyr, (in an earlier manifestation as Tiwaz), may well have been the Great God of the North, a role that Odin has today. Some evidence certainly points in this direction (like an arrow from the Bronze Age). I have long felt that this take-over represents ancient memories the Precession of the Equinoxes and the promise to write this piece was a good opportunity to do some research.

An Old English Rune poem equates Tyr with Polaris, the North Star. Due to the wobble of the earth and Precession of the Equinoxes different stars take turns being the pole star (for periods of 2,160 years at a time). I see the Tyr rune as the arrow that points to the North Star of an earlier era. When the spinning night sky shifted, Tyr lost his bearings or prominent position and a new god, Odin, took over his rulership.

Our star constellation Ursa Major (Big She Bear) was viewed in Scandinavia as karlavagnen (Swedish for the wagon of the old man). In some areas this "old man" was Odin and in others it was Thor: 'Karla-Þórr' or Old Man Thor, an affectionate appellation.

Second arrow

The second window is a personal one: I often bring Tyr into my work with sacred art students. Tyr is best known for sacrificing his arm when the wolf Fenris was tied up, because an ancient prophecy informs us that if Fenris runs free, he will devour the world. The gods deceived Fenris by asking the dwarves to make a magical fetter called Gleipnir, and Tyr put his arm in the wolf's mouth, as false insurance, while the fetter was being tied. Tyr lost his arm and Fenris will not break free until the end times of Ragnarok. This explains why Tyr is sometimes called The Leavings of the Wolf.

Odin makes sacrifices on his quest for personal knowledge: he loses one eye and hangs on the world tree for nine nights to gain the knowledge of the runes. Tyr makes his sacrifice on behalf of the community, to ward off the end times of destruction. This would have cost him dearly, in integrity as much as physically speaking. Tyr raised Fenris as a pup. He broke his oath to get Fenris securely chained.

Tyr therefore is a great teacher when it comes to *sacrifice*. The word comes from Latin and literally means making sacred (and that was done by offering to the gods).

Self-sacrifice is demanded of most human beings in the course of an incarnation on earth. Commonly we grieve our losses with anger and resentment. We lose sight of the fact that we committed a profoundly sacred act. In the reframing of that we find a wellspring of healing. Tyr can be called on to help people realise where sacrifices made were a sacred act that safeguarded or preserved the life or the well-being of vulnerable others. Those choices were in service to *Life*.

Tyr is a flawed cosmic hero, one could say. He broke an oath but saved our world from premature destruction. Tyr can help us see that some of our life choices were compassionate: those of "a hero, rather than a victim". In reclaiming that piece, we regain personal power and we gain peace of mind.

WEPWAWET

Melusine Draco

Not to be confused with Anubis, Wepwawet was originally a war god from Upper Egypt and his name means 'Opener of the Way'. He was depicted as a jackal or as a jackal-headed man sometimes carrying a mace and bow, suggesting that he 'opens the way' before the king in battle since his image is frequently depicted atop the standard that led the armies, with the cobra-uraeus of Wadjet in front of him. A prominent deity dating back to pre-dynastic times he held pride of place in the Egyptian religious order. The customary and regular representations on a range of royal objects bear testimony to his important association with pharaohs down the millennia. Wepwawet played many roles and was venerated not merely as a funerary god, but also as one who assisted the king, not only in warfare, but when he celebrated the Heb Sed jubilee festival, too.

Wepwawet was the local deity of Lycopolis, which mean 'the city of wolves' in Greek and as a result was associated with Anubis, who similarly was a jackal-like deity, eventually being considered to be his son. It is often difficult to distinguish Anubis and Wepwawet as coming from a different species but the strongest evidence lies the Greek names for their respective cities, that of Anubis being Cynopolis, 'dog city', while that of Wepwawet was Lycopolis, 'wolf city', where 'wolf' likely means almost any wild member of the dog family. And whereas Anubis usually appears in his customary black, Wepwawet is often coloured blue-grey as we can see from his famous portrait at the Temple of Set I at Abydos.

Wepwawet was also known as the funerary deity, portrayed as a jackal-headed man in military attire and carrying weapons in his hand, being seen as one who opened the ways to and protects the deceased through the Underworld. By the Old

Kingdom he was popular throughout Egypt, but later absorbed by Khentyamentiu, a god of the Abydos necropolis. In the Pyramid Texts, however, it states that Wepwawet was the one who has separated the sky from the earth, perhaps as the 'opener of the sky' and as such, helped the deceased through the frequently dangerous paths to the afterlife, clearing the way to the final judgment of the dead.

Although frequently paired with Anubis in connection with protecting the dead, Wepwawet also had his own independent identity, as well as important cult centers at Asyut and Abydos. Inscriptions from Lykopolis attest to his status as a popular local god. On his own, Wepwawet often appears as a standing jackal or standing jackal-headed god; when he and Anubis are paired in funerary art, the two gods are typically shown as identical seated jackals facing each other. Wepwawet is also more likely than Anubis to be depicted standing, rather than recumbent, and in pairs, rather than singly, a trait some Egyptologists argue as indicating that the animal depicted is indeed a jackal, inasmuch as mated jackals hunt in pairs, unlike dogs and wolves which hunt in packs.

The iron instrument used in the 'Opening of the Mouth' ritual is called in Pyramid Text Utterance 21 'the adze of Wepwawet', indicating that historically Wepwawet may have preceded Anubis in this role. In PT Utterance 210 *the Wepwawet-jackal which emerged from the tamarisk-bush* is a symbol for the resurrected king. In Utterance 482, it is said of the deceased king that 'you shall become Wepwawet', while in Utterance 535 it is said of the king that *'your eyes have been given to you as your two uraei because you are Wepwawet who is on his standard and Anubis who presides over the God's Booth* [i.e., the embalming tent]." *Uraei* are fire-spitting cobras and hence light the way in the darkness, a function obviously related to that of Wepwawet insofar as the uraeus accompanies him on the king's standard.

Interestingly, an epithet given to Wepwawet as a 'disrupter', literally 'loud of voice' is typically a negative trait in Egyptian literature and often associated with Seth. The same stela, which depicts Wepwawet harpooning a crocodile, reveals the god as having picked up some of the more *positive* aspects of Seth associated with his defense of the solar boat against the serpent of chaos and disorder, Apophis.

From this we can see that Wepwawet is a far more complex character than may have been previously thought. His pre-dynastic antecedents suggest that he was another casualty of the social and religious upheavals at the end of the Pyramid Age. A surviving story tells that Wepwawet was born at the sanctuary of Wadjet, the sacred site for the oldest goddess of Lower Egypt and consequently, Wepwawet, who had once been the standard of Upper Egypt alone, formed an integral part of the Unification of Egypt.

YAHWEH

Laurie Martin-Gardner

Once little more than the national god of Samaria (Israel) and Judah, today Yahweh is the One True God to approximately three billion Jews and Christians worldwide. From just another warrior deity among hundreds in the Late Bronze Age, Yahweh eventually transcended his humble beginnings to become the creator of the cosmos and the only god in heaven.

The historical beginnings of Yahweh have been lost to us, but many scholars have concluded that he was originally a warrior god worshiped in Midian in present day Jordan. For the faithful, however, Yahweh is eternal and has existed since the distant and mysterious beginning. From his word and will alone, he brought order from chaos, set into motion the mechanism of time, and crafted the earth and life in all its many forms. But we are not actually introduced to Yahweh in the Bible until the book of Exodus when he appears to Moses in the form of a bush that burns but is not consumed. When asked for his name, Yahweh reveals to Moses the four Hebrew consonants YHWH, "I Am Who I Am" (Exodus 3:14), and instructs him to use that name when sharing his word with the Israelites.

Up until that miraculous moment on Mt. Horeb, the god of the Bible was referred to as El or the variant Elohim. To the faithful, El was simply another name for God. But it is very likely that the god of the patriarchs was not Yahweh but El, the Canaanite High God. To account for this, after revealing his name as Yahweh to Moses, the Biblical writers have him assure Moses that he was the god of his forefathers but that his true name had not been known to them. Regardless, Yahweh became the name of the god that led his chosen people from Egypt and into the promised land of Canaan.

After being delivered from the clutches of Egypt, the Israelite people entered into a covenant with Yahweh. He would provide them with protection and blessings, and they in turn would serve no other gods before him. The existence of other gods was unquestioned at this point, but for the Israelites, none would be worshiped but Yahweh. But they soon found that it was difficult to stick to such a restrictive covenant in the polytheistic lands they inhabited. Slipping repeatedly back into the ways of their ancestors, the Israelites soon discovered that the same Yahweh that led them to military victory could, and would, lead armies against his own people as punishment for transgressions against their jealous god.

But Yahweh would not remain the vicious and petty god of the early Jews. A transformation began to take place that would set him apart from, and above, other deities. While pagan gods had always been experienced and understood through their relationship with the natural world, Yahweh inhabited a wholly different and unreachable realm. And he was no longer confined to the world of the Israelites. His glory filled the entire world, and with it, his authority to rule all peoples.

This transition, however, was not easy or peaceful. Entire tribes were decimated in Yahweh's name. Temples and altars to old gods were destroyed, their priests murdered, and the dead desecrated. There would be no god but Yahweh, no matter what the cost. And though it took hundreds of years, eventually the Yahwist zealots won and the Jewish faith swept across the known world.

Somehow, despite all the atrocities enacted in his name, Yahweh became a symbol of hope to his people. During their exile in Babylon (6th century BCE), the Israelites clung to him and depended on his grace to see them through their hardships. Just like the pagan gods of old, Yahweh transformed to fit the social climate of the time. The Israelites, cast into a foreign land, clung to his familiarity and his promises. They no longer needed the warrior. They needed a savior, and so Yahweh became a beacon of light in their long darkness. In Babylon, Judaism was born, and the world (quite literally) would never be the same.

Whether Yahweh was once a pagan god, an amalgamation of gods, or wholly unique to the Israelites, it is impossible to overstate his importance in the development of the modern world. Wars have been fought, nations have been conquered, and lives have been forever altered under the banner of Yahweh. And although much evil has been perpetuated in his name, great acts of kindness have also been inspired by his glory and his promises still fill hearts with hope and gratitude. Yahweh is far too complex to sum up in a few short paragraphs. And unlike many of the ancient gods that came before him, Yahweh's story is far from over.

YAM

Laurie Martin-Gardner

Perpetually angry and unreasonably violent, Yam was the powerful Canaanite god of the sea and rivers. He was the turbulent sea that crushed ships and pulled men down into a watery grave. He was the swollen river that burst from its banks swallowing crops and strangling livestock with his unwavering grasp. His home was beneath the waves, in the deeps of the primordial waters, and so he was also the untamed chaos present from the beginning of time. He was both feared and revered, not only among the Canaanites but the Phoenicians and Egyptians as well.

Much of what we know about Yam, also called Yam-Nahar, comes from a series of fragmentary texts discovered in the ancient port city of Ugarit in modern day Syria. Known as the Baal Cycle, the text chronicles Yam's rise to power within the Canaanite pantheon and his eventual downfall. The saga begins with Yam's father and the Supreme Canaanite God, El, choosing Yam to rule as the king of the gods. El mistakenly believes that Yam will be a benevolent and worthy ruler but almost immediately Yam is overcome by a need for more power. The texts read, *"Fearsome Yam came to rule the gods with an iron fist."* Yam forces the other gods to labor for him until they can no longer endure his tyrannical rule. The gods cry out to Athirat (Asherah), El's wife and the Great Mother Goddess, and she agrees to plead their case to Yam.

After dismissing every gift and favor Athirat offers to him, the goddess decides that the only thing she has left to offer is herself. Yam accepts, and Athirat returns to the assembly of gods to tell them the terms of Yam's agreement. All the gods agree to this plan except one. Baal is outraged by both Yam's demands and the willingness of the other gods to offer Athirat, their mother, to the monstrous god. He swears to kill Yam himself, a plan which Yam soon discovers. The Sea God then sent emissaries to the heavenly court with instructions to show no respect to El, or the assembled gods, and to demand that they hand over Baal for punishment. While the gods were content to surrender Baal to his adversary, he would not go quietly and challenged Yam to combat. Using specially made magical weapons, Baal struck Yam between the eyes and the tyrant fell in defeat. Baal proclaimed himself king and tossed Yam out of heaven and back into the sea.

In some versions of the tale, Yam is not so easily defeated. He repeatedly interferes with Baal's reign, bringing calamity to heaven and earth again and again. Some scholars see this as representative of the annual cycles of rain and drought common in Canaan. Similar tales were told throughout the ancient world. Although clearly the villain in the Baal Cycle, Yam was not considered an evil or bad god. Yam was simply a violent force of nature that needed to be revered and reckoned with. We know very little about how Yam was worshiped, but we do know that he was considered worthy of the same sacrificial rites that were offered to El and Baal. According to Greek sources, the Canaanite-Phoenicians often adorned the prows of their ships with a horse head in an attempt to appease Yam who, like the Greek Poseidon, was associated with horses.

Like most of the major Canaanite gods, Yam eventually became a part of the Hebrew faith as well. Although he did not play as prominent a role as El or Baal, references to Yam can be found throughout the bible. Long associated with the mythic sea serpent Lotan, Yam became the seven headed sea monster Leviathan. Just as Baal had defeated Lotan, the Hebrew god Yahweh was depicted as defeating Leviathan in a triumph of order over chaos.

Perhaps it was inevitable that Yam's association with the sea serpent would become equated with the infamous serpent in the Garden of Eden that tempted Eve with the forbidden fruit. As the idea that the serpent was actually Satan began to develop, Yam/Leviathan was again transformed into the role of the Devil. The Canaanite Yam is hardly recognizable by the end of the Hebrew Bible.

It is unquestioned that Yam was a brutal and rigid deity who abused his power and his fellow gods. But for the Canaanites, he was just another aspect of an uncontrollable world. He could sink ships or see them safely to port. He could flood the fields or entice them to grow. By venerating Yam, the Canaanites hoped to win his favor and avoid his wrath. And although he was eventually twisted into something dark, the true Yam gave meaning to the misfortunes often suffered in the land of Canaan.

ZEUS

Scott Irvine

The king of all the gods, Zeus is probably the most recognised god today after Yahweh and Allah, having survived through the age of the monotheistic gods by blasting his thunderbolts from the texts of the classical Greek myths. His reign began as the Babylonian empire fell into decline in Asia and the power of the gods began migrating into Europe around 3,700 years ago. The last ice age was slowly retreating north-westwards leaving a lush fertile continent in its wake covered in deep forests, gentle valleys and fresh rivers west of civilised Asia. The eastern gods bought farming and city life with them making Zeus the European version of their air god Enlil. Arriving in the west, Zeus brought with him a beautiful Phoenician princess called Europa; the conquest of the opposite sex was a game he liked to play when he could escape the jealous gaze of his wife Hera. Zeus fell in love with Europa the moment he set eyes on her and stole her heart by disguising himself as a powerful white bull encouraging the princess to sit on his back. As soon as Europa was safely on, Zeus bolted towards the shore, swam across the Mediterranean Sea to a deep cave in Crete setting up a secret love nest with his lover and new family.

The classical myths reveal that when Zeus was born, his mother Rhea had to hide him away in a cave in Crete to protect him from his father, the god of time, a Titan called Cronus. Cronus knew of a prophecy revealing that one of his children will wrestle power from him so he ate them as soon as they were born. When Zeus was old enough, he forced his father to spew out his siblings before exiling Cronus and the rest of the Titan's to a subterranean prison off an island in the west fulfilling the prophecy. Zeus went on to rule over the Olympian gods of Eastern Europe with two of his brothers, Poseidon, the god of the sea and Hades, Lord of the underworld. As god of the air, Zeus ruled everything in and under the sky including the sun, moon, the planets and the stars. His name means 'brightness of the sky' and was the force of nature that brings storms and floods to the parched farming lands and rains to replenish springs and rivers while hurling thunderbolts at his enemies and those that disobeyed his wishes; upset him at your peril.

While sat on a cliff looking out to sea, watching cargo ships sail by on the horizon and closer in the small fishing boats busy chugging up and down the channel I was suddenly aware that I was at a place where the forces of Zeus, Poseidon and Hades met, constantly eroding the coastline and changing the landscape forever. I felt the sea air on my face and listened to the waves crashing against the bottom of the cliff, its impact felt under the ground where I sat. At the time I was contemplating on taking a gap year from working, living off my savings to write a book about my pagan beliefs. Was it the combination of the wind and the breakers mixed with the cries of the gulls whispering 'do it' into my head, a voice that seemed to come from the elements. It revealed that Zeus spoke for his brothers and the story of the earliest primeval feminine forces recorded, needed to be told. I had to step out of the modern world for a time to reveal secrets from the ancient past. The whisper told me everything will work out fine and not to worry, the universe would take care of my needs.

Zeus is a distant god but approachable for the female cause, after all women were his life's pleasure. One of his daughters, Eris was angry for not getting an invite to a royal wedding attended by all the important Olympians. In revenge she presented Zeus with an apple as a gift for the most beautiful goddess in the world. It put the king of gods in a very difficult position, he couldn't choose between his wife Hera, his sister Athena and his daughter Aphrodite; he would get considerable grief from the two he did not pick as the fairest of them all. The most diplomatic thing he could do was pass the judging onto someone else, a young prince from Troy called Paris. The Trojan chose Aphrodite who promised him any woman his heart desired which happened to be another of Zeus's daughters, Helen who unfortunately for Troy was married to a Spartan king who wanted her back leading to the destruction of the great city and scattering its royal families around the globe with some migrating west to found Rome and Britannia. In Rome Zeus became Jupiter and in Britannia, he became the Dagda.

Hail Zeus
Yay Zeus
Je Sus

You might also like...

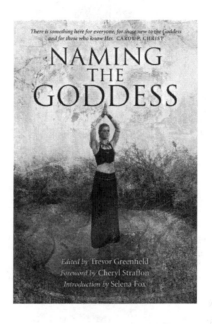

Naming the Goddess

A must read for those old and new to Goddess
Annabell Alexander

978-1-78279-476-9 (Paperback)
978-1-78279-475-2 (ebook)

**MOON
BOOKS**

PAGANISM & SHAMANISM

What is Paganism? A religion, a spirituality, an alternative belief
system, nature worship? You can find support for all these defini-
tions (and many more) in dictionaries, encyclopaedias, and text
books of religion, but subscribe to any one and the truth will evade
you. Above all Paganism is a creative pursuit, an encounter with
reality, an exploration of meaning and an expression of the soul.
Druids, Heathens, Wiccans and others, all contribute their insights
and literary riches to the Pagan tradition. Moon Books invites you
to begin or to deepen your own encounter, right here, right now.
If you have enjoyed this book, why not tell other readers by
posting a review on your preferred book site.

Recent bestsellers from Moon Books are:

Journey to the Dark Goddess
How to Return to Your Soul
Jane Meredith
Discover the powerful secrets of the Dark Goddess and
transform your depression, grief and pain into healing
and integration.
Paperback: 978-1-84694-677-6 ebook: 978-1-78099-223-5

Shamanic Reiki
Expanded Ways of Working with Universal Life Force Energy
Llyn Roberts, Robert Levy
Shamanism and Reiki are each powerful ways of healing; together,
their power multiplies. *Shamanic Reiki* introduces techniques to
help healers and Reiki practitioners tap ancient healing wisdom.
Paperback: 978-1-84694-037-8 ebook: 978-1-84694-650-9

Pagan Portals – The Awen Alone
Walking the Path of the Solitary Druid
Joanna van der Hoeven
An introductory guide for the solitary Druid, *The Awen Alone* will
accompany you as you explore, and seek out your own place
within the natural world.
Paperback: 978-1-78279-547-6 ebook: 978-1-78279-546-9

A Kitchen Witch's World of Magical Herbs & Plants
Rachel Patterson
A journey into the magical world of herbs and plants, filled with
magical uses, folklore, history and practical magic. By popular
writer, blogger and kitchen witch, Tansy Firedragon.
Paperback: 978-1-78279-621-3 ebook: 978-1-78279-620-6

Medicine for the Soul
The Complete Book of Shamanic Healing
Ross Heaven
All you will ever need to know about shamanic healing and how to
become your own shaman...
Paperback: 978-1-78099-419-2 ebook: 978-1-78099-420-8

Shaman Pathways – The Druid Shaman
Exploring the Celtic Otherworld
Danu Forest
A practical guide to Celtic shamanism with exercises and
techniques as well as traditional lore for exploring the Celtic
Otherworld.
Paperback: 978-1-78099-615-8 ebook: 978-1-78099-616-5

Traditional Witchcraft for the Woods and Forests
A Witch's Guide to the Woodland with Guided Meditations and
Pathworking
Mélusine Draco
A Witch's guide to walking alone in the woods, with guided
meditations and pathworking.
Paperback: 978-1-84694-803-9 ebook: 978-1-84694-804-6

Naming the Goddess
Trevor Greenfield
Naming the Goddess is written by over eighty adherents and
scholars of Goddess and Goddess Spirituality.
Paperback: 978-1-78279-476-9 ebook: 978-1-78279-475-2

Shapeshifting into Higher Consciousness
Heal and Transform Yourself and Our World with Ancient
Shamanic and Modern Methods
Llyn Roberts
Ancient and modern methods that you can use every day to
transform yourself and make a positive difference in the world.
Paperback: 978-1-84694-843-5 ebook: 978-1-84694-844-2

Readers of ebooks can buy or view any of these bestsellers by
clicking on the live link in the title. Most titles are published in
paperback and as an ebook. Paperbacks are available in traditional
bookshops. Both print and ebook formats are available online.

Find more titles and sign up to our readers' newsletter at
http://www.johnhuntpublishing.com/paganism
Follow us on Facebook at https://www.facebook.com/MoonBooks
and Twitter at https://twitter.com/MoonBooksJHP